Bruce Grobbelaar

Bring on the Clown

WITH BOB HARRIS

COLLINS
WILLOW

The Publishers would like to thank Umbro International Ltd for their help in supplying much of the kit and many of the props for the photographs reproduced in this book.

William Collins Sons & Co. Ltd
London . Glasgow . Sydney . Auckland
Toronto . Johannesburg

First published 1988
© in text Bruce Grobbelaar and
Bob Harris 1988
© in drawings John Ireland 1988
© in photographs William
Collins Sons & Co. Ltd

All colour and black and white photographs by Bob Thomas

BRITISH LIBRARY CATALOGUING IN
PUBLICATION DATA
Grobbelaar, Bruce
Bring on the Clown
1. Soccer – Anecdotes, facetiae, satire, etc
1.   Title II. Harris, Bob,
796.334   GV943.2

ISBN 0 00 218278 5

Filmset in Melior by
Rowland Phototypesetting Ltd
Bury St Edmunds, Suffolk
Printed and bound in Great Britain by
Butler and Tanner Ltd, Frome, Somerset

Contents

Barmy Baby –
Childhood Reminiscences

Bruce David Grobbelaar is such a silly name that the only dafter profession I could have followed other than that of goalkeeper would have been that of a juggler, for my surname, translated from the Dutch, means clumsy. There are a few managers around who would happily endorse that translation and wish I had gone into the circus instead.

That's not as unlikely as it sounds, either, because one of my relatives played the saxophone in a circus band. But I was always going to be in sport of one kind or another, and football was just unlucky to be the one I opted for instead of cricket, rugby union or baseball.

The dark continent may have many deficiencies with brother killing brother, black killing black, and black and white killing each other, along with repressive governments of all colours, but synonymous with southern Africa are sun and sport. Every child, whatever his colour or creed, is born into the perfect sporting environment, although it must be said that some have better chances of excelling than others. And that is why the world chose to punish every South African with sporting sanctions rather than with total economic or political embargoes.

But enough of the heavy stuff. Sport was in my blood from the moment the midwife smacked my bum in the Durban maternity hospital on October 6, 1957, for she probably had one eye on me and the other on the 3.30 at the adjoining Greyville Racecourse in Durban. It wasn't very thoughtful of my mother, Beryl, and father, Hendrik (no prizes for guessing which side of the family was of English stock), to allow a budding international sportsman to be born in a country where I would be banned because of the apartheid policies, but they compensated for that by their own sporting backgrounds. Mum was a top hockey and softball player while my Dad was an all-rounder, good at most things but especially baseball, badminton, tennis and, of course, as a goalkeeper in football.

Dad was good enough to play in goal for Rhodesia against Malawi at the Glamis Stadium in Salisbury, and it was a tragedy that such a sporting man should eventually have his left leg amputated as a result of Burgher's Disease.

The sad thing about it was that he might have halted the disease had he listened to the doctors and stopped drinking and smoking. He eventually died of gangrene in December 1981. By then the family had become known as the 'Hopping Grobbelaars', because he was the third of the family to suffer a leg amputation, with Uncle Willie undergoing surgery after falling down a mineshaft. I almost joined the clan when, as a four-year-old, I tried to stop a bike on which I was a passenger – by sticking my little leg through the spokes on a downhill run. No wonder we are called the Grobbelaars. Clumsy is an understatement!

Instead I survived intact to develop my sporting instincts. Perhaps God had looked down favourably on me on that occasion because I had just been performing in a play at the Tree Tops Nursery School and was still dressed in my costume as the angel Gabriel. Considering the dangerous nature of my chosen work, I have continued to be one of the great survivors with – touch wood – very few injuries until recent years. Even then I've suffered only minor ailments after five successive seasons for Liverpool without missing a game. Before that I chipped both elbows playing indoor soccer in the States; dislocated fingers keeping wicket at cricket; suffered tennis elbow through not warming up before pitching at baseball; sprained an ankle in pre-season practice falling down a hole in Durban; broken my nose in Rhodesia – and cut my chin in a Liverpool bar!

Maybe it is old age creeping up on me, but I have almost matched that paltry collection in the last two seasons with a bad stomach injury sustained at Wembley and a broken elbow suffered at Old Trafford. I do like the big stages, don't I? I also flaked a bone in my ankle – the same one I damaged in Durban – and now and then I have to click it back into place. The elbow caused the most problems because I had to have it pinned. I didn't mind too much because it helped my golf swing, but after I'd had the pin removed, the stitches burst open every time I played.

Scarcely had that cleared up than I was put out of action by a wicked, over-the-top tackle. No, not Norman Whiteside or Gary Thompson, not even Andy Gray – but Liverpool's own Steve McMahon in a five-a-side match, when he left two holes in my leg, one of them right down to the bone. I was furious, threw down my bib and stormed off. The club and manager, Kenny Dalglish, wanted it kept a big secret and I missed three successive games. Then I couldn't get my place back from my understudy, Mike Hooper, for the fourth as he kept four successive clean sheets. Those Liverpool five-a-sides are often tougher than our League games; perhaps that's where we gain that extra competitive edge. But leave the poor goalie alone chaps, even if he is a better outfield player than some of you!

Back to my childhood, a time when the last thing on one's mind is injury. I suppose the big difference between growing up in England and in southern Africa, where I shuttled between Rhodesia and South Africa, was that

A goalkeeper needs to be
a bit of an acrobat

instead of watching out for cars and lorries when you were kicking about in the back streets, you had to look out for lions and other fierce animals.

Dad worked for the Rhodesian Railways, which was a sporting blessing in disguise if ever there was one, for it meant automatic membership of the very well-equipped Raylton Sports Club. Both Mum and Dad were active, not only in competing in everything but also in fund raising, and as a tot my favourite sport was World Championship wrestling, which was staged as a fund-raising exercise. My parents' contribution was to run the hot-dog stall, where I'd sit under the trestle table, munching away at sausages until it was time to find my seat to watch the Masked Tornado tangle with Big Singh. These guys were brought in from everywhere, including Britain and the States. Just as much fun was the next day, when the adults would clear up the ring and the chairs while we kids picked up the litter, handing in 'finds' like spectacles, false teeth and lost underwear, while keeping any cash we found.

The Raylton Club also introduced me to a different form of wrestling which is even better known world wide and practised not so much in the ring as in dark corners – more often than not between members of the opposite sex. This mixed sport also went on at our Braii Uleiss (barbecue), when I witnessed so many 'bouts' in the garage, behind the car, in the garden and the house that I grew up thinking it was normal behaviour. It was no surprise as I grew up to

learn that Rhodesia had one of the highest divorce rates.

It would have been funny except that my handsome father was often the main feature of these unscheduled matches, and I could see the heartache it caused my lovely Mum. Sadly, it was therefore a shock to no one when the gipsy in Dad took over and the two separated to go their different ways.

On the more active side of sport, I gradually progressed from bean-bag racing, egg and spoon and – my forte – the sack race to the real business of goalkeeping. Having played in that position himself, Dad was delighted by my interest and bought me a set of goalposts to put up in the garden so that I could hurl myself about to my heart's content. It was the perfect set-up, climate and surroundings. When I was bored with goalkeeping, or if I could find no one to shoot in, there was always an alternative at the Afrikaner family's house next door, where I would take off my shoes and socks to tread the washing in a big bath, just as the French used to do when treading the grapes for wine. It was great fun but it made my feet soft, which wasn't always conducive to good, barefoot football.

It also meant I kept up my Afrikaans language. I had to speak like a Boer when I was with my father and his family, and English when I was with Mum's side. Later in life I made good use of my linguistic skills in America, when I used to go around with the famous Dutch international, Ruud Krol, while we were both with Vancouver Whitecaps in Canada. Although Afrikaans is closer to Flemish,

we could understand each other enough to have a conversation without the subject – usually a pretty girl – knowing what we were talking about.

My goalkeeping skills helped me in an unexpected area when I moved on to junior school in Rhodesia, where I added swimming and springboard diving to my growing repertoire of sports. The twisting and turning off the one-metre board came easily, and when I was eleven years old, I came fourth in the Mashonaland Junior Championships. I also represented the Mashonaland District at football, even though I was a couple of years younger than the rest and looked ridiculously small between those posts when we lost to the Boer farmers and Afrikaners from the mountains who played for Manicaland.

The next year, when I was an inch or so taller, we gained our revenge by winning the trophy. How I enjoyed my first taste of success! It was about this time that Dave Russell, coach

A goalkeeper needs to be master of his penalty area

for Salisbury Callies, saw me cavorting barefooted in a local park and asked if I fancied joining a proper club to play organised football. Mum said no until Dave persuaded her by offering to pay my fees.

It was my first experience of multi-racial football, for though the Callies were all-white and almost all-Scottish in background, we played against black teams. This began to open my eyes to the disease of apartheid when, pre-viously, I had taken it for granted that the coloureds and the blacks were in-ferior in everything. Sport, more than anything else, helped to break down the barriers as we began to mix socially, even taking our opponents to the neighbouring Hellenic Club for a swim, much to the chagrin of the older mem-bers.

Life was great in those days as I also began to develop a taste for travelling as well as sport. There were frequent trips to South Africa to play for the Rhodesian Fawns against the Spring-boks at both cricket and baseball, and those long journeys by train or lorry to the Northern Transvaal were great adventures. Also travelling to play the boarding schools of Plumtree and Guinea Fowl at rugby, we quickly be-came seasoned train riders, although not in the orthodox way.

My knowledge of the engines through my father's work stood me in good stead for, to pass the time, we had competitions to see who could ride the roof of these monsters. I knew all the footholds and ledges and how the rail-road workers made the climb on stationary engines. No one was hurt but it was extremely silly and very unfair on the teachers who had the unenviable task of looking after 80 to 100 restless young men. There was a strict ban on smoking and drinking on the way out, though we were allowed to share the odd beer on the way back.

The rugby matches were well con-tested, for the Boers lived for their rugby and there was nothing these growing young men liked better than to bang a few townies' heads together. Well, perhaps there was, but we had no black players so they made do with us. I usually played fly half in these rugby matches, but learned more about the facts of life when I stupidly volun-teered to stand in for the absent hooker. I was gouged, kicked and punched, surrendering only when I thought I had broken my back in the middle of a collapsing scrum.

Better fun and much safer was raid-ing the school kitchens. They would feed us with stuff we didn't like during the day, and to compensate, we would help ourselves after lights-out. My favourite food as a kid was peanut but-ter and syrup sandwiches, creamed sweetcorn and a poached egg on toast or good old-fashioned baked beans on toast. I have to admit I was a fussy eater; at least, I was until I went into the army. There was no time for fads there, when you had to make do with cooked mapani worms, flying beetles, locusts, snake steaks and birds (doves, pigeons or anything that flew), though I always drew the line at earthworms, cen-tipedes, slugs, caterpillars and the poisonous green locust. No wonder that, these days, I will eat anything that is put in front of me.

Those trips also taught me not to

play cards. Not that we had much money to lose; in fact I had to find a sponsor to pay for my travels. Instead there would be forfeits for the losers, and I frequently had to pay my dues by running naked through the train, that being one of the milder punishments.

Baseball is a different ball game altogether – if you will pardon the expression. There was even less money about for that, so we used to make the long 1,000-mile journey in the cheapest way possible, travelling with our sleeping bags in the back of a covered lorry. There would be five of us in each of three battered trucks, which were covered in canvas and open at the back to fumes and dust. If we were lucky we would sleep in a motel, but if not it was under the stars. Being in such a confined space, we naturally found this means of transport even more boring than the train, although there were diversions, such as the coach's pretty little daughter who used to sit at the front, becoming more beautiful by the boring minute.

Petrol stops also offered a welcome break from the monotony of the country roads on the way to Sasolburg. It was a chance to go to the loo or to chat up the coach's daughter but, most of all, it was an opportunity to get lost! Invariably we would set off in our mini-convoy minus one of the players. It happened to me once when I lingered a little too long in the washroom near the South African border. I sat on a pile of old tyres for fifteen minutes before they came back.

We did well, beating a few of the top South African teams, and though we failed to win the trophy, when we were invited back the next year we had to split up into three groups to make sure we were not too strong. We won the competition outright, anyway.

The next year it was held in Johannesburg, where we were billeted out with our opponents. I stayed with a Japanese family with two brothers, the pitcher and the catcher in the Transvaal team. While the rest of us had to rely on secret signs to tell our catcher what ball we were throwing, they simply had to speak to each other in their own language. Remember I was a finicky eater, so sushi and chopsticks were a bit of a culture shock. I couldn't wait to get out and buy myself a hamburger.

An even bigger shock came when I ran away from my mother's home to see my father and his new wife 100 miles away in Inyazura, where I was promptly volunteered to play for the local police team against a farming community team named Odzi. The pitch was a field cut out of the bush; because there were no changing rooms we all changed on a bus, and half the players were barefooted.

The game progressed without incident until the quiet of a sultry African afternoon was rent by the screams of a woman, who emerged from the tall elephant grass around the edge of the pitch, screaming, 'Amaai, Amaai'. No wonder she wanted her mummy, for as we turned to look at her sprinting across the pitch, clutching a small baby under one arm, we saw a fully grown lion loping casually after her.

Everyone scattered in different directions; I followed Dad's advice to get on the bus, and one of the watching

policemen radioed for a tranquilliser gun. The sleeping lion was soon carried 20 miles or so back to the National Park from where it had come, with no one the worse for the experience.

A more common sight in and around Inyazura were some very unusually coloured monkeys called vervets, characterised by the fact that their private parts were an incredible, electric blue. Many people had them as pets and would show them off by taking them for walks on a long lead. The brighter the blue the bigger the status symbol, while all the young men about town yearned for a car in monkey-ball blue.

We had one with the brightest coloured testicles anyone had ever seen and he made a wonderful watchdog, because of his link to the witch-doctors, who used monkey's tails as switches. Sadly, after he had bitten my brother's finger, we had to replace him with a real watchdog, who was poisoned within weeks by burglars trying to break into our house.

Even the monkeys were scared of other monkeys. A white international rugby player who lived not far away had terrible trouble with rampaging baboons on his farm, so he went out with a gun, shot one and stuck it up on a stake in his field like a gruesome scarecrow. It worked. The other baboons stayed well away.

Sometimes my schoolteachers reckoned they were teaching a baboon, for while my sport continued to progress my academic life left something to be desired, and was not improved by detentions, strappings and the other usual chastisements. Football was beginning to gain the upper hand on the sporting front, so much so that I signed on as a schoolboy professional with Salisbury Callies, and when the first-choice goalkeeper, former Hibs player Walter Lowrie, went down with an injury I was plunged into first-team football.

These were very definitely dreams of things to come, for I was on the winning side as we came through both the quarter-final and semi-final of the BAT Rosebowl. Along with my great mate, Graham Shearer, I was looking forward to playing against Mashonaland United, a black team from Bulawayo, in Salisbury's Rufaro Stadium. I felt sure I would play, especially when Lowrie turned up for the final training session in his suit; but, having watched us work out, he declared himself fit. I still expected to play until that night in the team hotel, when the manager told both Graham and me that we would not be in the team because our inexperience could cost us the Cup.

To say I was upset would be to understate the whole affair. When Shearer and I took our places in the stand along with 498 other whites in a capacity crowd of 50,000, we were somewhat noticeable – both cheering for the opposition. We rowed with the chairman, shouted abuse at our teammates, and went wild when a long-range shot from Gibson Homela bounced past Lowrie for the softest of goals. We were out of our seats and dancing for joy.

You have no fear of the consequences at that age, but after the game I was treated like a leper. I naturally couldn't stay with Callies after my be-haviour, and my headmaster also indicated that if I did not leave school I would almost certainly be expelled. So, faced with a choice like that, I felt that the time had come to join my mother and step-father in Bulawayo. Callies put me on loan to Matabeleland Highlanders and I was on the train that same night.

Deciding it was time to knuckle down, I was determined to do better at my new school, Hamilton High School of Bulawayo. I did well for the school team and found that the absence of girls made studying easier. God knows what would have happened had I not tried, for I came twenty-seventh out of thirty with my form master writing on my report: 'An outstanding goalkeeper for the first team, but he has made little effort to catch up and must concentrate on his school work rather than his football.' A sentiment echoed by the headmaster who added: 'I have admired his goalkeeping ability but he is wasting his time in the classroom.'

That was the end of my childhood, for obviously I was not going to add to my earlier passes from Mount Pleasant High School in Salisbury, and the time had come for me to go out into the big wide world and seek a living. Again the timing was perfect, for a club named Chibuku, owned by a brewery, came in with an offer to buy my registration from Callies, and even offered me a job in the brewery. Everyone, particularly my poor Mum, was happy with the outcome, except the supporters of the Highlanders, who felt that I was more than just a simple deserter, for all their supporters drank Ingwebu beer.

Once again, though, my progress was

Goalkeepers tend to last longer
than outfield players

anything but smooth and manhood did not come easily. My international début was marked by a broken nose playing against Dynamos in the Gwanzura Stadium right in the heart of the black township of Harare. Bleeding profusely, I was rushed to hospital in an ambulance. I should have realised the hospital was not all it might have been when another casualty and I were asked to fill in a form before we could see a doctor. Sure enough, they told me that my nose wasn't broken, which was pretty bad for me, but the other guy had broken his writing arm!

By the time my Mum picked me up, I was having to hold my eyelids open, with my nose located somewhere beneath my left eye, and no one else in any doubt as to what Oliver 'Flying Saucer' Kataya had done to my hooter with his boot.

It had to be rebroken and set three days later. So I left the next morning to play for Mashonaland in the Inter-Provincial Championships with a cast over my nose, looking like one of Oliver Cromwell's roundheads. You don't have to look too closely to see that the effects were fairly permanent.

My career with Chibuku also ended quickly when the entire team were involved in a mass punch-up with, of all clubs, my old team the Callies. I didn't like what I saw, took off my boots with a gesture of defiance and left the pitch, returning to play out the second half when order was restored. But afterwards I told the manager, Jack Meagher, that that was my lot, and as I left the club to pack my few belongings in my little mini I could hear the irate manager yelling that I would never kick another football as long as I lived.

There was only one place to go from there – the army. So on July 7, 1975 I voluntarily enrolled with C Company, 147 intake. Now I really did have to grow up for, before long, I was literally fighting for my very life.

Over the Top

Football is always a great source of humour because of the wide range of characters not just on the pitch but on the terraces and in the dressing-rooms as well, lending themselves to stories that may not always be true. These belong strictly in that category.

• Glasgow Rangers's millionaire manager Graeme Souness was turning on to the motorway in his Silver Cloud Rolls Royce, heading for England to sign another couple of international players, when a battered red Ford Cortina came sliding into his rear end. Souness, furious, left Gerry, his chauffeur, in the car and approached the culprit on the slip-road hard shoulder. The door of the Cortina flew open and out jumped one of the Queen's Park amateurs, saying, 'Sorry, sorry it was all my fault and I'll make good any damage.'

'What the hell were you doing?' demanded the still-irate Souness.

'Look,' said the amateur pointing to his car, 'I lost my concentration. The telephone rang just as I was changing the tape in my video and, at the same time the telex machine started going.'

Souness was immediately interested and, forgetting his anger, peered into the back of the beaten-up Cortina. Sure enough, there they were: telex, telephone, video machine, even a cocktail bar. Impressed, he waived all thoughts of compensation in return for the name of the garage who had fixed it up and, scrapping his trip, told Gerry to take the car that day to the garage to have it fitted out.

A fortnight later Souness was pulling on to the same motorway when he spotted the red Cortina parked on the hard shoulder and shrouded by steam. He immediately got his driver to pull in behind, jumped out and rapped on the misted window which slowly opened to reveal the red, perspiring face of the young footballer.

'Remember me?' asked Souness. 'I'm the guy with the Rolls you ran into the other day.'

'I thought we had settled all that,' said the young man.

'No problem,' replied Souness. 'I just wanted to tell you I've got the lot now –

Some believe that it is a goalkeeper's job to entertain the crowd

telephone, telex, television, bar, everything.'

The youngster looked at Souness in disgust and spat out: 'You mean to tell me that you got me out of the sauna to tell me that!'

● Having been lucky enough to play in most parts of the globe, I know for myself that football is a world-wide game, so I was not surprised to hear of the shipwrecked sailor washed up on a remote island in the Pacific. After recovering, he went off exploring and, sure enough, he found a nubile young Girl Friday who insisted on ministering to his every whim and requirement. On the first day she insisted that he lay in a hammock, being fed with exotic fruits while he regained his strength. On the second day she produced a wonderful, refreshing rum punch, and on the third day she staggered the sailor from Liverpool docks by giving him a 200-pack of Benson and Hedges cigarettes. By this time the sailor was beginning to think he had found paradise and was convinced of it when, on the fourth day, the girl smiled at him, wiggled her slender hips and queried, 'Sailor like to play game?'

'Wonderful,' replied the Scouser leaping from his bed. 'You've got a football as well!'

● Professional football is becoming so commercial these days that all top clubs have three strips . . . one for home games, one for away games and one for televised games.

● I used to play football with the wife, but after the children were born I had to give it up because she didn't bounce too well.

● My wife Debbie and our daughter Tahli were looking around Hamley's of London last Christmas when Tahli spotted a superb but very pricey dolls' house, complete with lighting, furniture and all accessories. Enchanted, she asked Debbie if she could have it, only to be disappointed by being told that it was far too expensive. Tahli thought for a minute before suggesting, 'We could always sell Daddy to Tottenham Hotspur.'

● Local derbies in Scotland have lost a handsome source of income since the sale of alcohol has been banned at the grounds. They used to make a fortune on the empties.

● Talking about the Scots, there was the unfortunate punter who showed that he was afraid at Ibrox as the bottles flew past his ears.

'Dinna worry,' said his neighbour. 'Remember what they used tae say in war aboot the bombs? You'll no get hit unless yer name is on it.'

'That's what bothers me,' said the frightened fan. 'Ma name's Johnnie Walker.'

● Everton are having a big supporters' club membership drive. They've already driven away hundreds of their members.

• Tranmere once had a goalkeeper nicknamed Cinderella because he was always so late for the ball.

• One of the reasons I decided to become a goalkeeper instead of playing outfield was because when I was a youngster I was told that one of the most important assets for any footballer is the ability to pass a football. Sounds far too uncomfortable to me.

• Always remember that the referee is absolutely essential in football because without him we would have no one to blame for our defeats.

• I telephoned my old club, Crewe Alexandra, to ask what time their game against Tranmere kicked off as I wanted to bring a crowd of visiting friends from Zimbabwe. They asked me what time we could make it.

• I am not saying that Crewe are struggling for fans these days, but when we arrived and asked for two at £5, the gateman asked if we wanted defenders or forwards.

• We arrived inside just in time to hear the announcer giving the crowd changes.

• Crewe's manager, desperate for a change of luck, telephoned Kenny Dalglish for some advice on how they could improve their basic skills. Kenny, always ready to help, told him how we practised by dribbling and running between traffic cones, helping our control and speed. A week and two defeats later,

he went back on the phone, asking if Kenny had any more ideas. Kenny told him to keep at it and not to lose heart.

'It's all right for you,' moaned the Crewe manager, 'but the cones beat us twice as well.'

• When a star First Division footballer was killed in a tragic road accident, the whole country went into mourning, except for the young, unfeeling, lacking-in-talent reserve, who saw his chance of making the team. He picked the day before the funeral to approach the distressed manager, asking if he could take the dead man's place. The disgusted boss replied: 'That's the best idea you've ever had. I'll see if I can arrange it with the undertaker.'

• When the crowds are small, the barracking from the terraces seems that much louder and that much more distinct. It is always the referees who suffer most on these occasions, and one unfortunate official finally allowed the remarks to get to him. Striding off the pitch and signalling a policeman to join him, the referee pointed to the foul-mouthed offender and said: 'I've been watching him for the last half hour.'

'I thought so,' replied the unmoved fan. 'We could all see you weren't watching the game.'

• The late Sir Stanley Rous delighted in telling the tale of the day a man in the crowd offered him a white stick, saying in the traditional manner: 'You must be blind, referee.'

'What did you say?' demanded Stanley in his best menacing voice.

'Deaf as well,' responded the quick-witted punter.

● Language can be a problem when foreign coaches take over a team, even when they all supposedly speak the same language. There was the famous incident in Rhodesia when the English coach told his players that they would be playing a powerful team and he wanted everyone in defence. He was staggered when half the team rushed over and stuck their heads through the railings.

● Our local amateur club are looking for a new treasurer. I remarked to the skipper that I thought they had appointed a new treasurer only a week before.

'Yes,' he answered gloomily. 'That's the one we're looking for.'

● When the brain of the Liverpool team boasted that there was nothing he did not know about football, I stumped him by asking how many holes there were in our goal nets at Anfield.

● A lot of cheating goes on in football, no matter who is playing. There was the classic case of the Liverpool Rabbis taking on the Liverpool Priests in a challenge game. The Rabbis were so desperate to win that just before the game they signed on a new goalkeeper – Rabbi Southall. But they still lost, with the Liverpool Priests scoring twice through Father Dalglish and Father Barnes.

● The epitaph on the tombstone announced: 'Here lies the body of a great referee and an honest man.' Strange that, they don't often put two bodies in the same grave.

● A particularly fiery First Division manager was given much of the credit when his team came back from a three-goal deficit to win 4–3 in a thrilling, fighting finish. The football writers were desperate to know what had been the theme of his half-time text, but no one would say until the captain sheepishly admitted that the great man was nowhere to be seen until seconds before the re-start, when he put his head round the dressing-room door and said: 'Well girls – shall we go?'

● My old mate Graeme Souness was called up again by the Scottish Football Association's disciplinary committee after being reported for abusing the referee. When the referee was presenting his report the churchman on the committee asked the official what Souness had said, leaving out the swear words.

'Nothing,' replied the bemused referee.

● Liverpool have always been strict on timekeeping, and when our team comedian arrived half an hour late, an irate Ronnie Moran rushed up to him, pointing at his watch, and saying: 'You should have been here at ten o'clock.'

'Why?' asked the comic. 'What happened?'

● When David Fairclough played for Liverpool he sat on the bench so often that they called him the Judge.

● There was more than one wife around Britain pleased when English clubs were banned from Europe. However, one in particular was delighted – and understand-

ably so – following a wild night of celebrations in Estoril after Liverpool had beaten Benfica. As the Scotty Road Supporters' Club wound their way back to Lisbon Airport for the flight home, they came across the recumbent form of one of their members. Needless to say they looked after their own, picked him up and poured him on to the special charter flight where he remained quietly unconscious until landing at Speke. Concerned about his condition, two of his mates decided to take him home to his wife. After knocking vainly on his front door for ten minutes, they were searching through his pockets for the keys when a neighbour leaned out of a window, calling: 'It's no use hammering on their door – they've gone to Portugal for a fortnight's holiday!'

● Any Scouser kid who has a football is guaranteed to be the most popular on the block. On the way out of Anfield the other day I heard some ragged urchins asking at a door, 'Can Bobby come out to play, Mrs Smith?'

'No he can't,' replied Mrs Smith. 'He's having his tea.'

'Well,' countered one of the little lads, 'can his football come out to play then?'

● They reckon that the kids in Merseyside are christened by dipping them in the river. If they come out red they're Liverpool, if they come out blue they're Evertonians.

● A slightly overweight Press man, playing in a charity match, was enjoying the luxury of signing autographs before the game for some youngsters who wouldn't know Steve Curry from a Chicken Madras. The Press man, enjoying the attention, told his young audience: 'The moment the ball is played into me, my brain responds instantly, commanding my legs to sprint towards the passer to be there first, my foot to control the pass with one touch, my body to swivel and shoot accurately into the top corner.'

'What happens then?' asked a wide-eyed youngster.

Contemplating the fact that he was about to be found out when the game started, the Press man answered: 'Then my body says "Who – me?"'

● Bill Shankly once said that football isn't a matter of life or death but something far more important. That's what they think in Liverpool. I have a neighbour who wears Liverpool's colours all day long, reads nothing but the sports' pages in the *Liverpool Echo* and never misses a game, home or away. His wife took all she could before grumbling with some bitterness: 'I think you love Liverpool Football Club more than me.'

Looking up from the paper with some contempt, he replied, 'I love Liverpool reserves more than you.'

● An important question in Liverpool is whether there is life after death. They needn't worry. There is indeed football in the hereafter, because I heard about a challenge match between the angels and the devils. The angels were quick to take up the challenge to play on a neutral cloud, convinced they would win because they had all the healthy, fit clean-living footballers in heaven. Satan, with a knowing wink, replied: 'Yes, but we've got all the referees.'

● With so many Scots in the Liverpool team it was no surprise to see two of them almost come to blows on a trip to Israel. Having stood at the hotel bar for five minutes waiting for someone to come in and buy them a drink, one eventually turned to the other and asked: 'What'll ye be drinking?'

'A large gin and tonic.'

'Just tell me the drink and I'll decide how much of it ye'll have,' was the sharp response.

● Frank Clark, manager of Leyton Orient, was driving to training one morning when he spotted a young black youth in a side street messing about with a football. Mesmerised by the lad's natural skill as he kept the ball off the ground, Frank pulled in and watched until he could restrain himself no longer, jumping out of the car and asking the lad his age.

'You've got the lot, son,' enthused Frank. 'Come and sign for the Orient and you can play for us on Saturday.'

'Forget it,' replied the youngster, tucking the ball under his arm and leaving. 'Don't you think I've got enough problems as it is?'

● Everton's brilliant Welsh goalkeeper, Neville Southall, was beaten so often in Merseyside derby matches by his fellow countryman, Ian Rush, that one day when they passed each other in the Scotty Road, Ian nodded and Neville dived straight into a pillar box.

● Footballers are not known for their humility, but I overheard one in a Liverpool hotel bar who really pushed the boat out with a new girlfriend, boring her with the story of his life, his games for England, the cups he had won and how he was going into politics when he retired. Suddenly aware that she was rapidly becoming more and more nauseated, he stopped with the words: 'But that's more than enough about me.' Taking her hand and moving closer, he went on, 'Let's talk about you. How did you think I played this afternoon?'

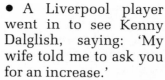

● A Liverpool player went in to see Kenny Dalglish, saying: 'My wife told me to ask you for an increase.'

'Right,' replied Kenny. 'I'll ask my wife if I can give you one.'

● They're nuts about football in Liverpool and some of them are just nuts. There was this Liverpool supporter who went to see a psychiatrist, another big Reds fan.

'First,' said the medical man, 'I'm going to test your reactions with word association. What has smooth, round curves and becomes difficult to control at crucial moments?'

'A football,' came the reply.

'Good,' approved the psychiatrist. 'And what comes to mind when two arms go around your waist?'

'A rugby tackle; a foul.'

'And what do you think of when you see a pair of firm thighs?'

'A top footballer.'

'Fine, fine,' said the psychiatrist, smiling. 'You are as sane as I am – but you would be surprised at some of the silly answers I get!'

● Danny, the pretty blonde wife of Liverpool's former captain, Graeme Souness, took everything as it came, even her husband's reputation as something of a hard man. When they telephoned her from Anfield with the news that they were bringing him home with a suspected broken leg, she responded: 'Oh, yes, and whose is it this time?'

● When Graeme took over Rangers, he gave his players a terrible rollocking after losing to bottom-of-the-table Hamilton Accies. Noticing one of the reserves sitting in a corner barely able to conceal his mirth, Souness suddenly swung on him, pointed a finger and snapped, 'I don't know what you find so funny – you can't even get into the team.'

● Sometimes the gates were so poor when I was at Crewe that the turnstile man would ask the last one in to lock up after him.

● Bill Shankly, Brian Clough and the Bishop of Liverpool were passing a pleasant afternoon in a rowing boat in Hyde Park, discussing the meaning of life. It was a hot day, and after a while, Shanks asked the other two if they fancied an ice cream. Stepping over the side of the boat, he walked across the water, bought three ice creams and returned the same way without a word about his extraordinary behaviour. An hour later Brian Clough climbed over the side of the gently bobbing boat, also returning over the lake five minutes later with three soft drinks. The Bishop was astonished, but not to be outdone by these two football managers he volunteered to buy the next round, gingerly stepped over the edge . . . and promptly sank to the bottom.

As Shanks and Cloughie peered over the edge, Clough asked Shanks, 'Bill, do you think we should have told the Bishop about the stepping stones?'

'What stepping stones were those?' responded Bill.

● Bobby Robson tells the story, with emphasis on the word story, that when he took over as England manager from Ron Greenwood, his predecessor told him that in the top left-hand drawer of his desk at the Football Association headquarters in Lancaster Gate he would find three envelopes. When he lost his first game and felt the pressure of the nation, he should open the drawer, take out the top envelope marked 'one' and open it.

Sure enough, the first England defeat brought down the wrath of the gutter press on the head of the new England manager, and after going through the newspaper files, he remembered the envelopes. Opening the top one, he read, 'Call a Press conference and blame the whole situation on the lack of decent players I left you and how you have to rebuild from scratch.'

It worked brilliantly and gave the

manager breathing space until the pressure began to build up again after another couple of defeats. This time he had no hesitation in opening the second sealed envelope, which read, 'Call a Press conference and blame it on the system, the lack of preparation of your teams, the absence of help from club managers and the shortage of time with the players before games.'

Again the criticism turned to understanding sympathy and once more the manager had time to gather his thoughts, replan and try to build a winning team. Things went well until the inevitable happened and the team hit the wall again. As the cries for the manager's head grew ever louder, he reached for the third and final envelope. Opening it eagerly, he read, 'Take three envelopes, number them one to three and write in the first. . . .'

- Chelsea's former manager John Hollins knew he was in trouble when, during his summer holidays, he heard that he had been named Bell's Manager of the Month for July.

- At Goodison Park they arrested a pickpocket trying to put season tickets into people's pockets.

- Anfield has a rather imposing sign over the players' tunnel that reads 'THIS IS ANFIELD'. In direct contrast, I noticed that the sign over the players' entrance at Goodison Park reads 'NO BALL GAMES TO BE PLAYED AROUND THIS AREA'.

- Why aren't there any Everton lift operators in Liverpool?
  They can't remember the route.

- Why do Everton supporters have pock marked faces?
  From learning to eat with knives and forks.

- The waiter in the Liverpool Pizza Hut asked the Everton supporter if he wanted his Four Seasons Special cut into four pieces or eight? The Everton supporter replied:
  'Just four, I don't think I can eat eight.'

- Did you hear how the Everton supporter got concussion drinking water?
  The toilet seat fell on his head.

- What do you get when you cross an Everton supporter with an ape?
  A retarded ape.

- How do you break an Everton supporter's finger?
  Kick him in the nose.

- The two Everton players discovered the joys of horseriding and rushed off to the stables every day after training. They even bought themselves horses, but the only thing was that they couldn't tell one from the other. They thought they had solved the problem when one of the players cut a couple of inches off his horse's tail, but then his mate's horse caught his tail in the stable door and they were back to square one. Finally, they decided to measure the two nags to settle the issue once and for all. It worked. They discovered that the white horse was six inches bigger than the black horse.

- One of the Everton players read so much about the evils of drinking that he gave up reading.

Sometimes a few get passed

• The Everton centre forward boasted that he could run the 100 metres in seven seconds. This was too much even for his team-mates, who pointed out that it was more than two seconds quicker than Ben Johnson's world record.

'Ah,' said the striker, tapping the side of his nose, 'I know a short cut.'

• One of the Everton players was rushed to hospital when he suffered a splinter from the substitutes' bench. They called in a brain surgeon.

• When Everton were going through one of their bad runs and trailing a long way behind Liverpool, they called in a psychiatrist who, after several days, diagnosed: 'They do not have an inferiority complex – they *are* inferior.'

• When Everton first qualified for Europe, one of their defenders confided to his room-mate that he had never flown before and was worried about the effect on his ears of the pressure in the cabin. His friend, who had been to Majorca for his holidays, told him that he found chewing gum a big help. When the team landed in Italy, he asked his mate if the chewing gum had worked.

'Yes,' replied the first player. 'But how do you get it out of your ears?'

• The Football Association have been taking dope tests for years. Everton players always passed with flying colours, but there was one who stayed up all Friday night studying for his urine test.

● One of the Everton players came round to my house in Heswall collecting jumble so that the club could buy a new player. He was so fascinated with the lion's head hanging on the lounge wall that he asked if he could go in the next room to see the rest of it.

● There was another of their players who thought the English Channel was another name for BBC 1.

● The same player took his car into a garage because of an electrical fault on his starter motor. When the mechanic told him he had a short circuit he snapped, 'Don't just stand there like a fool, lengthen it.'

● I'm not saying that Everton players aren't intelligent, but it cost one of their players twenty quid to spend the night in an Amsterdam warehouse.

● Manager Colin Harvey became so exasperated by their stupidity that he called them together one day and began, 'Look lads, if we are going to catch up those lot from over Stanley Park, we are going to have to go back to basics. First things first: this is a football and . . . .'
'Hold on boss,' said the star centre forward. 'Not so flippin' fast.'

● The same player plucked up enough courage to ask Colin for an increase. Having prepared his case, he burst into the manager's office and said: 'I have been doing the work of three men all season and I reckon that I deserve a raise.'

'Sorry,' said Colin, 'I can't give you a raise, but if you tell me the names of the other two players I will fire them immediately.'

● Everton Supporters' Club invented the first million-pound lottery to raise money for the club. The winner got a pound a year for a million years.

● Four managers were having a confidential chat, and after a few brandies, began to talk about their private lives and their secret vices. The first confessed, 'I've got this bird on the side, little flat by the ground, wonderful relationship.' The second stunned his colleagues by admitting, 'I'm a kleptomaniac; can't help pinching things; house is full of hotel towels, club crockery, even trophies. I can't help myself.' Encouraged by the honesty of his friends, the third revealed, 'I am not only a secret drinker with gin in every cupboard, but I am a compulsive gambler as well.' They all turned to the fourth manager who shrugged his shoulders and said, 'Me? I sell gossip to the Sunday papers!'

● The directors of the northern club finally ran out of patience and sacked their manager when the team lost their tenth successive game and slumped to the bottom of the table. Having placed an advertisement in the local paper, asking for applicants for the vacant position, they were disappointed to receive just one reply from a man who said he would take the job only on condition they switched their home kick-off times from 3 p.m. to 2 p.m. so that he could catch his last bus to Todmorden at 5 p.m. With no alternative they reluctantly called him in for an interview, asked for his credentials and were staggered to hear that he had managed clubs all over the world, won every possible honour as a player, and had scored the winning goals in European Cup and World Cup finals. What is more, he claimed to have taught George Best all he knew about the game and discovered Denis Law in the Aberdeen backstreets. He would be delighted to take over 't' Rovers', but reminded the board that his last bus left the market at 5 p.m. and he would have to be on it. The board, thrilled, asked him to step outside for a minute while they confirmed his appointment. All were in total agreement apart from old George, who had sat in the corner listening to the goings-on with increasing disdain until he finally blurted out: 'The man's a bloody liar, a con man . . .. The last bus doesn't leave market place for Todmorden until 6.30!'

• The Irish goalkeeper had travelled over by ferry to talk to Liverpool about signing for them. Talks were long and protracted, broken off only because it was Tuesday and Liverpool had an important game that night. Paddy decided to walk to the game and on the way his attention was drawn to a fire in

one of Liverpool's many high-rise buildings. Out of curiosity he joined the gathering crowd and saw, to his horror, a woman standing on a ledge ten storeys up, holding an infant and screaming, 'Save my baby, save my baby'. No one knew what to do until Paddy stepped forward, calling, 'Drop the baby and I will catch him. Don't worry, I am Ireland's international goalkeeper and I am about to sign for Liverpool. Your baby will be safe with me.'

The anguished mother took some persuading until the situation became so hopeless that she sobbed her assent and relinquished her hold on the child, who floated towards the ground like a leaf in a gale. Paddy weaved from side to side trying to gauge the exact spot where the terrified child would land, moving from foot to foot to the accompanying gasps of the now-vast crowd. It looked as though he had got it all wrong until, at the very last moment, he hurled himself to his right and caught the baby in both hands at full stretch. But just as the mob were about to hail their new hero, their cheers were strangled in their throats as Paddy jumped to his feet, bounced the baby twice on the pavement and half-volleyed it down the street.

The Snake Man and Other Jungle Tales

Doe Herbst was what he sounds, a typical boorish Boer. A big, bad machine-gunner who put notches on his gun for everyone he killed; and if he could get close enough to them he would cut off an ear, put it on a string, and take them home to his farm in the Kahama Ruins where he kept them in a jar. His party trick was to eat his glass after he had finished his drink and, apart from ears, he also collected snakes.

Doe, like me, volunteered for service with the Rhodesian Armed Forces, although our motives differed somewhat. He had his problems. Not only had he served six months in a civilian prison for wrecking a bar in a drunken fight, but he was also lusting for revenge after suffering family bereavements and considerable damage to his farm at the hands of the terrorists.

A big man in every sense of the word, and a frightening figure when drunk, he didn't need his machine-gun to put terror in any opponent's heart. You call a man 'boss' on his farm when you see him lift bags of grain in his teeth to impress his hired hands.

At first he would go to the border to exchange cigarettes with the Mozambique guards, but after we had been bombed at our schoolhouse headquarters and shot at by snipers who killed his best friend, he wanted to go and gun the lot down. While the rest of us became caught in a trap and feared for our lives, he revelled in the action. After the bombing we had to abandon our tiny two-foot bunkers covered by a tent for proper six-foot-deep trenches, protected by sandbags and big enough to live and sleep in when necessary. This was when we discovered that our friendly machine-gunner had an affinity for snakes.

It could become cold at nights up in the Eastern Highlands where we had our camp, and our deep bunkers offered a little warmth, not only to us but also to the snakes. I woke up one morning, had a stretch and a scratch, and was folding up my sleeping bag when I felt something moving about inside. Sure enough a puff adder had crawled in beside me during the night. It was a good thing I was a sound sleeper and that we slept in our uniform and boots, because if I had tossed and turned I might well have stayed asleep for ever!

Doe came to see what the problem was and, discovering it was a snake, he calmly reached into the sleeping bag, pulled it out by its throat and stuck it in a hessian bag which he hung on a hook in his machine-gun bunker. Before long the contents of the sack began to grow, and Doe would scout around the schoolhouse for live mice to feed his new found pets.

On patrol we had to watch out for the boomslangs or tree snakes which hung like vines from trees; when you passed, they would drop on you, trying to fasten their big jaws on any part they could reach. You had to move quickly because once those hinged jaws gained a grip, they would be hard to shift. One of these boomslangs once made the dreadful mistake of dropping on Doe's neck as he wandered by. He simply reached up, yanked it off, stunned it and popped it in the sack, which was now hooked to his waist.

They all came alike to Doe. Green mambas, grass snakes and even a baby python, twelve feet long and with the girth of my wrist. That was the only one he couldn't keep in his sack. All the rest were lethal in one fashion or another and some got on together and some did not. Doe discovered which did or didn't by trial and error. When he went home he took the lot with him to his farm outside Bulawayo. He didn't talk about it a lot and he wasn't the sort you pushed, but we gathered that he would use them like guard dogs – if someone came calling whom he didn't like, he would throw one of his 'pets' out of the door. Another of his friends topped Doe's glass-eating party trick by biting the heads off the smaller snakes.

I have a lasting memento of Doe Herbst, which will remain with me to my grave. It is a tattoo on my left shoulder, depicting the Olympic rings and a single black rose, etched into my skin by Doe after one of the most frightening experiences of my life.

My stick of four men had to go off with others on a very hairy patrol. Aware that there were plenty of terrorists who would take advantage of the natural camouflage of the surrounding jungle and the tree-lined lagoon, we tried to relax with a dip in the water, two swimming while the other two stood guard. We cleaned our teeth with fine sand and washed with a pumice stone, rubbing freshly cut ferns into our skin afterwards. It was important not to become too squeaky clean, because if you did and stood downwind, you would be easier to pick out than a tramp at the Savoy Grill.

We then laid our ambush down in the valley, carefully selecting the killing ground that any moving terrorists would have to cross, propping claymore mines against trees to direct the blast towards them. We then settled back in the dark with one on duty while the other three tried to rest, attached to him and each other by a string tied to a toe – if anyone was daft enough to take off his boots – or more probably a thumb, so that a quick tug would silently wake everyone in one go.

The claymores were also supposed to be our alarm call, but the battery attachment malfunctioned so that the first we knew of the presence of terrorists was when my pal, Stooge Ayre, heard a rustling in the bush and there, six yards away from our hidden position, were a dozen of them – armed. A confrontation was unavoidable; if they had kept walking they would have trodden all over us. In an instant Doe was blasting them with his machine-gun, and after the smoke had cleared four terrorists lay dead and another two injured.

It was still an hour or two from first light and we knew that if we stayed where we were we would be dead men. Have you ever tried crawling backwards up a steep hill in full kit and carrying a rifle? It's not easy, but we cleared 50 yards in around 180 seconds. Within minutes our previous position was riddled with gunfire and nothing, not even one of Doe's smallest snakes, would have survived that fearsome barrage. There was no radio contact until the morning and there we crouched, frightened to our boots, except Doe who quietly puffed on a sweet smelling cigarette, cupping it in the palm of his hand to hide the glow. I still get the shudders and nightmares when I think about it – and people wonder why I wasn't scared of that penalty shoot-out in the European Cup Final against Roma in the Olympic Stadium. On this occasion my knees wobbled for real, and the shots aimed at me featured something a little more dangerous than a plastic-coated leather football!

That's why I celebrated in such an unusual manner. The Olympic rings were because I have always been a romantic about the concept of bringing people of all colours, races, cultures and creeds together in the name of peace and sport, while the rose is the flower of love and the black rose a flower of death. All very philosophical.

When I asked Doe to do it for me – I found him asleep in a hammock slung under a big lorry as though nothing unusual had happened – he gave me one of his whacky ciggies and a bottle of cane spirits, telling me to drink the lot and to come back in two hours' time. That, of course, was the anaesthetic.

Doe had his own tattoos – naturally including one of snakes wrapped around a heart – and that night he got a friend to draw two ducks flying in a friendly position with the inscription 'FLY UNITED'. I asked him what it had to do with the horrors of the previous night, but he was apparently unconcerned about that. The new tattoo was to remind him of a night back on the farm, when he had been enjoying horizontal recreation with a girlfriend. Her pelvis dropped, and they had been stuck in that uncomfortable position for two hours.

When Doe was in the army you never saw him walk anywhere without his machine-gun. He looked as broad as he was tall and was fanatical about a game of darts and booze. If you beat him on the dart board you had to keep on playing double or quits until he won. You didn't argue. Of the few who did, one went away and committed suicide. That, I thought, was going too far, but Doe quietly explained that this particular guy drove an armoured car and would kill indiscriminately – kids included. Doe, for all his many faults, loved kids of any colour.

He also knew that most other people liked them as well, so when we raided a village looking for terrorists, weapons or food stores he wouldn't follow the usual routine of beating information out of the villagers. Instead, he would find the newest baby from the youngest wife of the chief, take it into the bush, fire a gun in the air and come back covered in blood, looking for the next baby. He never needed a second, and having extracted the information he needed, the unharmed infant would be gently returned to the mother while he bandaged the self-inflicted wound he had used for the blood effect.

Doe was a tough man with a soft centre. One of the problems we faced in the bush was the ticks in the game reserves. Once they had a grip they were hard to shift with powders and creams, but Doe would casually burn them out with a lighted cigarette end. He eventually succumbed to a broken leg, suffered as we went in to help another stick under fire. Once the helicopter had landed as close to the top of the hill as possible, we dived out of one door and Doe out of the other, to give us covering fire. The only problem was that while we had jumped out on the top of the hill,

Doe went straight down a crevice, breaking his leg.

How do you replace a man like Doe in a war? We did with another Boer named Sarel Vermaak, who was every bit as tough as Doe and possibly an even better gunner. Remarkably Sarel began as a cook until some tough SAS Scouts spurned the usual queuing system and went to the front. When Sarel objected they threatened his health, whereupon he simply jumped the counter and flattened the trouble-maker with a single blow.

Flat feet or not, Vermaak was every bit as much a killer as Doe Herbst. He was also just as crazy as the rest of us. On his first patrol with my stick, we were under a new man, Lieutenant Jones, who, fresh out of school, wanted everything done by the book which meant, among other things, guard duty of two hours on and two hours off instead of each of us in turn having one hour on and three off. To his credit Lieutenant Jones took the worst shift of four until six. We waited and, sure enough, he nodded off to sleep. We took his boots and rifle, backed off into the bushes and waited until 6 a.m. before throwing small rocks to wake him up. He went beserk, screaming and crying and threatening to court martial the lot of us until he realised that, in army terms, his crime of falling asleep on duty, was the worst of the lot. After that he forgot the book, used his common sense and became a very good leader.

That rifle was all important. We were taught right from the start that whatever else we left behind we held on to our rifle. It was, we were told, our wife. We even had a saying:

'This is my wife' – pointing at the rifle.

'This is my gun' – pointing at the groin.

'This is for shooting' – back at the rifle.

'This is for fun' – back to the groin.

In other words, don't mess around with your wife – or anyone else's for that matter.

It wasn't only guns and terrorists we had to look out for. Animals were also a problem, like the lion who wandered into our operations room looking for something to eat. Suspecting that they were on the menu, most of the guys scarpered while another began to fire indiscriminately. He could have done more damage than the lion, who changed his mind and loped off back into the bush.

It was a good thing the lion wasn't as brave or persistent as a certain spotted hyena we ran into while involved in a bloody phase of our service in the Inyanga region. We had seen him earlier when we were selecting killing grounds and setting ambushes. Doe Herbst, who knew about these sort of things, told us to be careful to zip our sleeping bags right up to the neck. We couldn't light fires, couldn't talk and couldn't fire our guns because of the close proximity of the terrorists. Imagine the horror, then, when the hyena came back while we were trying to sleep and dragged off my friend Stooge Ayre, whose arms were stuck inside his bag. He was dragged some 400 yards before Doe smashed the dog in the teeth with the butt of his rifle,

casually remarking that had there been a pack of them we would have been in real trouble.

The animal you really had to look out for, though, was the rhino, and we bumped into two of those while on our initial training. Again it was poor Stooge who took centre stage.

The scene was set around Lake Mcilwaine, where we had been sent for a refresher course under the top tracker and former terrorist Corporal Bonnias. Being quite close to Salisbury, we were in more danger from tourists than terrorists. More often than not one of the soldiers would find himself distracted from the spoor laid overnight and would pounce on some unsuspecting family enjoying the sights or having a picnic. Once the short-sighted Corporal Power followed a car.

On this occasion, when a big lad named Palmer took himself off like a bloodhound on the scent, Bonnias wanted to know who the hell he was following as it certainly was not the trail he had laid the previous night. We thought it might be an elephant, but Bonnias quickly told us it was a big chipembere, a rhino. Stooge was sent on into the tall grass while the expert tracker stopped to give the rest of us a lesson in determining how fresh the trail was. He almost turned white as he realised just how new it was; we must have been seconds away from offering the rhino some toilet paper.

Meanwhile, Stooge, unaware of all of this, wandered off, head down, until he emerged in a clearing – between two snorting, pawing rhinos! He froze. Bonnias yelled for us all to climb trees while he ran at the short-sighted ani-

mals, waving his arms and bellowing at the top of his voice, which gave the frightened Stooge time to scramble up a tree. Once Bonnias saw him safe, he looked round for safety himself, finding that the only option open to him was a slender, bending sapling. The rhino took some time to focus, but when he did it was on our corporal. He immediately charged the fragile tree, sending Bonnias's rifle clattering to the ground, followed by anything else loose enough to be shaken free, but fortunately the sapling was pliable rather than dry.

Eventually the bored rhino and its beady-eyed, watching mate lumbered off, but as we began to climb down from our perches, Bonnias told us to stay where we were. They would, he promised, be back – and they were. Fortunately, rhinos, like elephants, are loth to destroy their natural habitat – and the trees in particular – so we all escaped unscathed.

Another animal unintentionally came to our aid when, during the same course, we were despatched beyond the tourists into the dry scrubland almost on the Botswana border. We were sent into this barren area for four days, armed only with our rifles, with one round up the spout and one full magazine of twenty rounds to be used if we encountered terrorists. The idea of shooting an SOS into the air was fine if the wind was blowing in the right direction. To test our initiative we were also given a single egg – but not to eat. We had to bring it back hard-boiled. Not so difficult? We had no water and there was no chance of finding any!

We devised a method of digging a hole two feet down, lining it with one of our combat jackets with a tin mug over the egg and another canvas combat jacket over the top. In the scorching heat the steam generated cooked the egg. We only got nine out of ten for that one as it left a ring on our jackets and we were told we should have used our caps instead.

The biggest problem was the lack of drinking water, the few drops of dew we gathered in our mugs overnight being hardly enough to wet the mouth. But then we met up with another couple from our section – farmer Piete Vanaart and Pete Springer – who had used one of their bullets to kill a young impala. They showed us how to skin it for the meat and then extract the bladder intact, leaving the contents to cool overnight. It sounds awful, but it was only slightly salty, and when you are as

thirsty as we were, drinking it was no problem. Some of our comrades were less clever and returned to base so dehydrated that they were rushed to hospital and put on a drip.

The answer was that if you treated it all like a competitive sport, you would come through. Organised sport, of course, was hard to come by once our induction had been completed, although while we were training we had rugby and baseball to keep us occupied. With nothing else to do, the whole troop would turn out for rugby matches, and they weren't averse to offering the odd helping hand — or should I say foot — as it was a land-mined area for the wingers down the touchline. They couldn't travel five yards without being tripped.

When the rugby season finished, I was asked to organise the baseball and put a team into the newly formed local league. I had just broken the Rhodesian record for Junior pitching with 19 strikes out of 21, and was delighted to find, during the trials, that the regimental captain was the best catcher, which offered me the rare chance of revenge for any incidents during the week. He often complained of raw hands. We weren't a bad team, winning our first three games and earning the nickname of the 'Army Animals' — because of the way we screamed at the opponents' first-base man every time we made contact with the ball — or the Llewellyn Louts (after the name of our barracks), because of the way we talked batsmen out with our snide remarks. We had no chance of winning the title, because we kept losing players who were posted away, or we would have to forfeit games because we were out on manoeuvres.

We were physically rough as well, which is not easy in baseball. As pitcher I would let the better batters have the odd bean ball aimed straight at the helmet, while their runners couldn't always be sure of keeping their limbs in one piece as we slid in to crunch legs; they were in particular trouble if they were caught in between bases. I suppose army sides are the same the world over, trying to prove their manhood.

It was the same in rugby but, somewhat surprisingly, we lacked really big men and everyone wanted to play in the backs. We lacked the manpower to be as rough as we'd have liked. The Company sergeant major told us we needed to show more guts and immediately brought in a number of Military Police, including a goffle known as 'King Rat'. He was a legend in his own

lunchtime and the fact that he was an MP was down to the old adage of setting a thief to catch a thief. He was for ever in the chokey, but would always escape. However, he never went far and we always knew exactly where to find him in the settlement.

Because of his escapades he was the longest-serving national serviceman in the army, but making him an MP gave

of keeping one of these half-castes undected in a cupboard for two days. They got their own back by pinching all the table tennis balls until there were none left to play with, although God knows what they did with them. We also played a lot of darts, because we could combine that not only with a few beers but also with extra-mural activities with the major's little red-headed daughter – until she was sent away to a convent.

him new responsibility, and he could express his authority on the rugby field. He was certainly tough and was one of the few men to get the better of Sergeant Major Duplessis, an army boxing champion who liked to use recruits as sparring partners. We certainly earned more respect when King Rat was in our pack.

The other popular 'sport' was the very racist practice of 'goffle kidnapping', with our unit holding the record

Our services were also in great demand at the local gymkhanas, where we shifted bails of straw, erected fences and acted as clowns to amuse the kids between rounds. No, that wasn't where I learned to keep goal!

Once in the jungle, the quality of organised sport dropped considerably. We would still have a kick-about when

I would keep goal, but the favourite was a rough, tough game called Bok-Bok, based loosely on the Eton Wall Game. We played it in the school hall, forming a scrum against the wall. I was never quite sure what the objective was, but it seemed to be to demolish the school – or the wall at the very least. We tried out of doors, where it developed into a sort of three-a-side rugby match, but there were too many broken noses.

I had not played an organised game of football for almost two years, so it came as a total shock when I was suddenly called up to join the Rhodesian national squad. And what made it all the more surprising was that the manager was none other than my old friend, Jack Meagher, the very man who had vowed I would never again play professional football in Africa. Our team, Chibuku, had been disbanded because of the war, and he had been put in charge of putting together a national squad to play against South Africa. After telling me I was in only because of exceptional circumstances, he expressed surprise when I told him I had not played for so long. God knows what he thought we and the terrorists had been doing in the jungles along the banks of the Limpopo River.

I was immediately relegated to third of three goalkeepers, which meant I was not even on the bench, so he could hardly raise any objections when I went ahead of the team to Durban to fix myself up with Durban City. I then travelled to Johannesburg to watch the international between the two banned FIFA countries, in which the home side scored seven past our goalkeeper Sibanda, a car-wash boy. I made my way back to barracks, only to be told I was under charge for going AWOL in South Africa instead of returning to Adams Barracks.

So here I was, on the very day I was due to be demobbed, facing a minimum of 100 days inside, further delaying my departure, which had already been put off twice by the government's extensions of compulsory military service. I sat handcuffed in prison for five hours, thinking of another three or four months of my life to be wasted. The only consolation was that it would keep me fit for football, this particular prison being noted for its strict regime, which involved a minimum of eight runs of the assault course before breakfast. Oddly, I was then double-marched to Major Taylor's door by my stepmother's second husband (if you can work that one out). The Major, whom I liked, was also on his last day at the barracks, having been promoted. He didn't even look up as he pronounced: 'I find you guilty.'

I gulped, waiting for the sentence, but need not have worried, for I was simply docked three days' pay. With great relief I heard him saying; 'The rest of your lot have demobbed. Report to the quartermaster with your kit and demob yourself. Thank God we don't have to go back into the bush with the likes of you.'

He knew it was all over. He had

known for ages. Which is why he put up with everything that went on in those final weeks, when we were paying the guards on duty to turn a blind eye as we unhooked the perimeter fence, already attached to convenient hooks on a tree. Half-a-dozen of the girls from the local town 2 miles away would be sneaked in to the barrack room, and hidden away in cupboards when the officer in charge made his rounds. It spoke volumes that no comment was made on the items of apparel that were still scattered around.

But then the girls always were the favourite sport, pastime and hobby of the armed forces with high security, fences and guards merely presenting added spice and challenge to the boy chases girl situation.

At one stage they even brought in women volunteers, who immediately earned the nicknames 'groundsheets' or 'sleeping bags', whether they deserved it or not. They were scarcely needed. Put a man in a uniform and there would usually be a girl around. Not that all the soldiers carried off that image. Corporal Farnie Cloette was a good stick leader but a disaster with the ladies. The moment he started talking to them he would begin to stutter.

When we were up in the Chimanimani Mountains we arranged a night out at the Chipinga Hotel, telling Cloette that there were a couple of girls asking specifically for him. Cloette was full of himself, but when the big moment arrived his confidence drained away, requiring him to go off and get himself drunk on cane spirits. By the time he returned, poor old F-F-F-F-F-

Farnie had missed out, with all girls taken. Most of the secretaries on base were looking for husbands with scrambled egg on their shoulders but, happily, the local girls, like us, just wanted a good time.

I was the luckiest of the lot, for I had a regular girlfriend named Jean Mac-Dougall, one of three equally beautiful sisters whom I met while driving a jeep on patrol in the Kateya Tea Estates. Jeannie was at a Catholic boarding school almost next door to our schoolhouse headquarters; naturally one of the favourite games of the men was to try to sneak into the dorms at night. However, the nuns were better patrollers than we were, and few made it past the security lights and eagle-eyed friends of Batman. Only four of us found our way in – straight through the front door! They had forgotten to patrol the obvious area.

Another of the intake to have a girl in the school was a crazy cockney named Julian Linson, who had a most lovely hippy girlfriend whom he would meet in the library. Julian was among those caught up in a mortar attack, which wrecked his right knee cap. Poor Julian, already a morphine addict, needed three times the usual dose to kill the pain, along with his bottle of gin topped up gently with lime. He was tough was Julian; he got up and walked away, and when he was in hospital he tried to show his disenchanted girlfriend how tough he was by flicking ash into the gap left by his missing knee cap.

It would be wrong to run away with the idea that life in the Rhodesian Army was all sport, whacky tobaccy and women. There was blood, death and desperate behaviour on both sides. We all lost friends and were lucky to come out of those jungles with our own lives, never mind our limbs intact. Maybe that is why I cannot consider football a matter of life and death. It isn't. Even at our high level it remains a sport, and when it ceases to be or I stop getting a laugh out of what I do – as well as my monthly pay packet – then I shall pack it all in and find something else.

You've Got to Laugh

Tn the occasions when football people gather over a beer or a meal, out comes the football — metaphorically speaking, of course. There are no worse gossips than the people in the game and the grapevine is so small that the stories, like the ones that follow, can be passed round in a matter of days.

Barmy

● They say all goalkeepers must be barmy. It is not always true, but bad luck does seem to follow us round. Just ask Graham Smith, the former Colchester and West Bromwich Albion goalkeeper. Spectators may have wondered why we tend to kick the foot of each post before the game. It is, simply, to adjust our boots. Graham went through the ritual, kicking one post and jogging over to the other — only to have the crossbar drop on his head!

High Speed

● Former Manchester United captain Martin Buchan was not only swift on the pitch but quick witted as well. As he left the dressing-room at Old Trafford he was intercepted by a local journalist, who tugged at his sleeve and asked, 'Excuse me Martin, can I have a quick word?' Without breaking stride Martin responded, 'Aye, velocity,' and walked on.

Baldy

● I know I would have got on with the old Queen's Park Rangers and Arsenal centre half, Terry Mancini, had we ever got to know each other. Not only was he balder than I but dafter as well. He once ran out in a magnificent wig, making everyone wonder who the new number five was, and he would claim that were his eyebrows longer he would sweep them over his head!

His classic was when he made his début for Eire, presumably qualifying

by thinking about going to Dublin for a long weekend. After standing through the long national anthem he whispered out of the side of his mouth that he hoped the Irish anthem was shorter and livelier. To frosty stares from all sides he was quietly informed that he had just been listening to it.

Clough Classics

• Brian Clough has always been very kind to me, particularly when the Press were giving me a bad time, though he has not always been as nice to other people in the game. However, even he has had his come-uppance now and again, and none better than from the former Everton manager, Howard Kendall, whom he had described as a young pup. Howard was asked for his response, but instead of countering the attack he simply said: 'I can't say anything – I'm a Hush Puppy.'

• Some of Clough's lines rank in almost the same class as those of Bill Shankly. Here are a few of my favourites:

On the sacking of his cricketing hero, Geoff Boycott, by Yorkshire he observed: 'I don't know of another club in history which finished bottom of the league, sacked its star player and left the manager in the job. The Yorkshire committee are guilty of the biggest whitewash I can ever recall.'

On players' intelligence: 'Show me a player who is thick and I will show you a player who has problems.'

On his former work-mate Peter Taylor: 'We pass each other on the A52 going to work most days of the week. But if his car broke down and I saw him thumbing a lift, I wouldn't pick him up – I'd run him over.'

He also had a go at his own fans for swearing and singing vulgar songs. Their response showed how much they thought of their manager. They held up a banner saying 'Sorry, Brian'.

Never afraid to criticise the establishment, he said of the Football Association, 'When they get in their stride they make the Mafia look like kindergarten material.' And of his board of directors at Derby County he said, 'There are seven of them and I wouldn't give you tuppence for five of them.'

The players don't escape either. His first million-pound buy, Trevor Francis, was a particular target, and he used to tell with glee how he made him fetch the tea. But even more humiliating was the day when Cloughie, due to present T.F. with the trophy for being the Midland Sports Personality of the Year, told him: 'I'll give you nothing until you take your hands out of your pockets.'

He also used to fine that tough defender, Kenny Burns, so often that he joked, 'He loves a little chuckle when I fine someone else.'

He never suffered fools gladly, and when asked to respond to a toast at a Leeds banquet he stood up and announced: 'I've been sitting here for two and a half hours and before I respond to anyone I'm going to the toilet.' When he returned, he told his surprised audience: 'If in future they want a puppet to get up and say something to please everybody, I suggested they invite Basil Brush.'

Not that he cared a jot what anyone thought about him. 'It doesn't matter if the players like or dislike you,' he said.

'It's when they respect you that they play for you.'

He also had an opinion on their wives, observing that 'footballers' wives should be like small boys – seen and not heard.'

It isn't that he always got it right. Ten years ago he promised everyone he would retire four years later, while earlier he had travelled with Peter Taylor to Southend to watch a player called Kevin Keegan.

'Too small and not experienced enough', was their decision on the Scunthorpe player, who cost Liverpool just £30,000 two years later.

But even when he did get it wrong, as he did at Leeds, he came out smelling of roses, picking up a reported £93,000 golden handshake for 44 days' work.

There were obviously facets that those Leeds players missed, for four years later he talked a woman out of a hunger strike. The woman said, 'He has given me a reason for living. I have never felt such tenderness. Mr Clough is truly a wonderful man.'

Also a philosopher, talking of his own profession he said, 'If a fox is completely brilliant, he finds himself a hole and hides. If his position is discovered, he is dug up and thrown to the hounds. But a football manager hasn't even got a hole to hide in.'

Sometimes players stayed for as short a time with Clough as he did with Leeds. The writing was on the wall for Asa Hartford when he remarked, 'At Ipswich he kept dashing off to mark Mick Mills. I got a message to him that if he wanted to meet Mills that badly I could arrange an interview after the game.'

He was always rude about John Robertson, criticising his drinking, smoking and clothes, but he liked him all the same, admitting grudgingly: 'He may be 30 and overweight, but he's the only player I've got who can control the ball.'

The man would insult anyone and two classics were: 'Football hooligans? Well there are 92 club chairmen for a start.' And: 'There are more hooligans in the House of Commons than at a football match.'

Right or wrong, love him or hate him, he knows what he is at. He happily accepted the nickname of 'Bighead' given to him by one of the posh Sunday writers, and when he applied for the job of Irish team manager he commented, 'It's easy enough to get to Ireland. Just a straight walk across the Irish Sea as far as I'm concerned.' That was in 1985; 20 years earlier, as manager of Hartlepool, he had already started to shape his image with the observation, 'In this business you've got to be a dictator or you haven't got a chance.'

That's Clough. I've always wondered how I would get on with him if he were my manager.

Cross-eyed

• Steve Coppell is another manager I respect. He almost made one of the worst starts as manager with Crystal Palace, after injury had forced him to surrender a brilliant career. Desperately needing a goalkeeper, he eventually tracked down one who fitted the bill, or rather the wage bill. Sitting across the table discussing personal terms, he felt there was something not quite right about the man facing him, but it wasn't until well into the interview that he realised his potential shot-stopper was cross-eyed. End of conversation; end of transfer.

• Coppell eventually wed his childhood sweetheart, Jane, much to the delight of his friends and family. Yet it was very nearly a disaster. On the eve of his wedding he bought a new suit in London before travelling up to Manchester to buy some shoes. Before going to bed at his parents' home in Liverpool, he proudly showed his mother the ice-blue suit and smart blue shoes, asking, 'Have you ever seen anything like these?'

'No,' said his mother. 'They are both left feet!'

So he set off for his wedding wearing one blue shoe and one black, desperately hoping that early-morning arrangements to pick up the right shoe would work. But even before the rendezvous with the shoe-shop manager, it was discovered that his grandfather, Eric, had left the wedding rings on the kitchen table, now some 20 miles distant. Jane had to provide a substitute for the service. It was only when he told Jane of the mishap that she revealed her own near-disaster. For when she had taken her wedding dress out of its wrappings, she found it was several sizes too large.

Still the fates were not satisfied. When they arrived for the reception at a hotel in Hale, Cheshire, the happy couple were greeted by a surprised manager who knew Steve well but had been fooled by the booking made under Jane's maiden name, in order to avoid publicity. The manager told Steve that by coincidence Manchester City skipper Paul Power had held his wedding reception at the same venue only the day before. He should have kept his mouth shut, for there on the tables were little posies of blue flowers, Manchester City's colours, and obviously something borrowed, something blue.

Bad luck even dogged them on honeymoon when they arrived at their Bermuda hotel. At dinner Steve was told he needed both tie and jacket, neither of which he had with him. They ate a romantic meal in the coffee shop.

46

Bob the Fat

● Whisper it quietly, but my co-author, Bob Harris, has also played a few games in goal for the Press team when they go off on their travels, often with hilarious results.

There was none funnier than his appearance for an 'England' side in the northern Spanish town of Bilbao. Bobby Charlton had gathered together a team of famous ex-players, including half of the 1966 World Cup side plus a few others like Don Howe and Bob Wilson. Unfortunately, Wilson refused to go in goal, even when the threatening Jack Charlton began to throw his weight around in the dressing-room before the game, berating the somewhat overweight, balding, bespectacled figure of Bob in his kit borrowed and begged from Peter Shilton, Joe Corrigan and Ray Clemence. It didn't help when Bob knocked back a finger trying to prove his worth with a pre-match save from Bobby Charlton.

Jack wouldn't leave off, even when the game against a talented and eager young team of Basques began. It was ironic that, despite the presence of all those stars, the photographs in the papers next day featured Bob and Bobby on their hands and knees looking for Bob's glasses, after a terrible Jack Charlton back pass had left the bold – or should that be bald? – goalkeeper with no option but to hurl himself at the surprised centre forward's legs.

● On another occasion, this time at Lanzarote in the Canary Islands, Bob Harris teamed up with Garry Birtles and Bryn Gunn in a scratch team against a team of super-fit athletes preparing for the Los Angeles Olympic Games. Despite the presence of the two pros, Bob's team was overrun, and he picked the ball out of the net at least ten times, blaming most of his failures on the athletes' secret weapon. No, not their superior speed and fitness, but the watching high-hurdler, Shirley Strong, sunbathing topless at the side of the pitch.

Shack

● Talking of 'golden oldies', brilliant but eccentric Sunderland winger Len Shackleton had little time for defenders, and even less for the shirt-tugging, spitting variety found at that time on the Continent. One day he encountered a foreign marker who insisted on tugging not only his shirt but his shorts as well, until the exasperated Shack took them off in the middle of the pitch, handing them to his surprised marker with the comment, 'If you like them that much, you keep them.'

Blarney

● Danny Blanchflower, captain of the Spurs double-winning side as well as of Northern Ireland, demonstrated his sharp mind long before turning his hand to journalism. The story goes that when the teams were being presented to the Duchess of Kent before the 1961 FA Cup Final, Her Royal Highness noticed that the Burnley players had their names on their track suits but Spurs didn't. Intrigued, she asked Danny why, as he presented the Spurs players to her and, without cracking a smile, he responded: 'We don't need name tapes, Ma'am. We all know each other.'

● It was also Danny who invented that much repeated remark while playing for the Irish. Asked why they were doing so well he replied, 'It's our new tactics. We equalise before the other side has scored.'

Since then there have been a few who get their retaliation in first!

● Which is just what the great referee Jim Finney did to Danny one day at White Hart Lane. Danny kept questioning Jim's decisions, eventually jibing him that it was only because he was showing off to the FIFA president and former referee, Sir Stanley Rous, who was sitting in the directors' box. Jim turned back and said quietly: 'Any more like that, Danny, and you will finish up sitting next to him.'

Who's Matt?

● Not everyone in the world loves our beautiful game, and even the most famous sons of football are sometimes brought down to earth by the uninitiated. It even happened to the great Matt Busby, right at the tail end of his playing days, just before the Second World War when he moved from Manchester City to join Liverpool and was called up.

Booked for the army, Matt made his way to the induction centre for his medical and to pass on his particulars. The busy clerk taking down the details not only didn't know who he was, but

also struggled to understand the Scots accent. When asked what his civilian occupation was, Matt naturally answered 'footballer', and was somewhat surprised, on joining his unit, to find that he was earmarked as a 'food boiler'.

Chairman John

● One of my great regrets is that I never had the privilege of meeting the late chairman of Ipswich Town, John Cobbold, whose *savoir-faire* and witty remarks made him one of football's great unsung characters.

He was the sort of man who, when Ipswich struggled near the foot of the First Division, offered manager Bobby Robson a new ten-year contract, showing that he not only had a good sense of humour but also knew his football. When asked at around the same time if there was a crisis, he responded: 'Crisis? The only crisis at this club is when we run out of white wine.'

Speaking to the media after Ipswich had landed a major sponsorship, he declared: 'It has been suggested that we will squander the sponsors' money on wine, women and song. That is absolute nonsense. We do not do a lot of singing at Portman Road!'

And he it was who remarked: 'Of course, we like competing in Europe. How else would we get our duty-free cigarettes?'

● England manager Bobby Robson never tires of telling stories about his late chairman, John Cobbold, especially the one about the day when John was invited to become president of the

South East Counties League. His acceptance meant that he would have to do something he dreaded: speak at a dinner in front of a great many notable football people. He and Bobby travelled down to London early for the event, so early that the bar was still closed. While waiting for him to open, he persuaded the amused barman to let them in for a drink, and he carried on drinking heavily with his guests, footing the bill as usual, listening to distinguished speakers like Lawrie McMenemy. In truth they had gone on for so long that when John stood up it was all too much. He swayed and gracefully sank to the ground, to be carried out to the biggest round of applause of the entire night.

• He liked a drink did John Cobbold and rumour has it that when Ipswich went to play Fiorentina and the group went sightseeing to Pisa, he was the only one who thought the Leaning Tower was straight.

• He was way ahead of the Football League, who changed the points from two to three for a win. John's adage was one bottle for a win, two for a draw and three for a defeat.

• He told an enquiring journalist that if things were going well Ipswich would have only two board meetings a year. 'Ah,' said the writer. 'But how many do you have when results are not going in your favour?' 'None,' replied John dismissively. 'There would be nothing to talk about.' True to his word, when Ipswich had a bad run under the successful Robson, he approached him after a series of five defeats and offered him a new three-year contract, saying to anyone who wanted to listen: 'Our manager's name is not written in chalk with a wet sponge nailed by the side.'

• He knew so little about other team's players that when Robson told him he was going to sign Mariner he thought he was going to buy a sailor.

• John and Bobby left a dinner before the speeches to relieve themselves. Afterwards Bobby went to the washbasins and looked on in surprise as the chairman made for the door. Catching him up Bobby remarked, 'Where I come from we were taught to wash our hands after going to the toilet.' Cobbold disdainfully retorted, 'Where I come from we were taught not to pee on our hands.'

• John Cobbold could be very *risqué*. After Ipswich had won the FA Youth Cup he invited the parents, landladies, scouts and everyone involved to a party, where it was suggested he might say a few words of thanks. He rose unsteadily to his feet, commanded attention and said: 'I hope everyone has had a good time and that the parents all go back to their hotel and have a jolly good time, so that in 18 years' time our manager Bobby Robson can win the FA Youth Cup again.' He brought the house down once more.

• But his humour could also backfire on him and the club he loved so much. John's great love after his football club was his donkeys. He began with two called Alka and Seltzer who produced a foal called Burp who, in turn, sired a donkey with his mother, aptly

named Calamity. All four were kept in his back garden where he could enjoy watching them through his French windows. One day he was looking at them lovingly when Bobby Robson arrived with Portsmouth striker George Ley and his wife in tow, trying to impress them enough to sign for the club. For no apparent reason John suddenly turned to his guests and asked George, 'By the way, you don't f––k donkeys do you?'

Needless to say Mrs Ley turned on her heels and walked out, taking George with her. Equally obvious was the fact that Bobby Robson never took a player to his chairman's house again – at least not until the ink was dry.

● John's father, Captain Cobbold, set the trend for the club's loyalty to their managers. The Captain was also chairman, and after appointing Scott Duncan as manager, had to go abroad to work. While he was away, all did not go well on the pitch and he felt obliged to send a cable to Portman Road stating, 'Buy Rimmer of Sheffield Wednesday', to which Duncan responded with his own cable, 'Will not buy Rimmer of Sheffield Wednesday'. Back came the Captain with: 'I insist you buy Rimmer of Sheffield Wednesday', provoking the reply: 'I insist I will not buy Rimmer of Sheffield Wednesday'. The now-angry chairman instantly cabled: 'Consider yourself sacked', but Duncan ended the correspondence with: 'Will not accept the sack'. The Captain knew then that he had a manager with a very strong mind, whose character paved the way for future managers – and the club have never terminated a contract since.

The Doc

● Tommy Docherty was and still is the king of the one-liners. People in the game often said he should be a comedian, and when circumstances forced him out of the game he did exactly that, through after dinner speaking. Here are some of his classics.

To Welsh international winger Leighton James: 'You're very deceptive son – you're even slower than you look.'

On midfield hard-man Remi Moses: 'Half a million pounds for Remi Moses? You could get the original Moses and the tablets for that price.'

On joining struggling Wolves: 'I opened the trophy cabinet and two Japanese prisoners of war fell out.'

And: 'We don't use a stopwatch to judge our golden goal competition – we use a calendar.'

On losing the Preston job: 'They offered me £10,000 to settle amicably. I told them they would have to be a whole lot more amicable than that.'

On politics in football: 'Henry Kissinger wouldn't have lasted 48 hours at Old Trafford.'

And: 'It's a rat race – and the rats are winning.'

On clubs: 'They're one of my old clubs (Preston). But then most are. I've had more clubs than Jack Nicklaus.'

And law courts: 'I've been in more courts than Bjorn Borg.'

On losing another job: 'When one door opens, another smashes you in the face.'

On Villa Chairman Doug Ellis: 'He said he was right behind me but I told him I would rather have him in front where I could see him.'

And directors in general: 'The ideal board should be made of up of three men – two dead and the other dying.'

And Manchester City chairman Peter Swales: 'He likes publicity so much that he wears a card round his neck saying, "In case of heart attack call a Press conference."'

On yet another dismissal: 'They sacked me as nicely as they could. In fact it was one of the nicest sackings I have ever had.'

In response to a player who said, 'I have a shock for you – I want a transfer': 'I've got a shock for you too – you can have one.'

On former Manchester United and England captain Ray Wilkins: 'The only time he goes forward is to toss a coin.'

In answer to a question at a coaching course at Lilleshall, 'What is the difference between technique and skill?', Docherty answered: 'Technique is to be able to control and pass the ball, skill is doing it with Tommy Smith's boot up your backside.'

It's Irish to Me

● A Belgian journalist, keen to interview Spurs' Nico Claesen after the European qualifying game against the Republic of Ireland in Dublin, was told by the little striker that as he was bidding to win a place in the Spurs Cup Final team, he would be off at the crack of dawn to catch the early flight back to training in London. If the journalist wanted a lengthy discussion he would therefore have to travel back with him.

Dutifully the writer returned to his smart Dublin hotel and booked an early morning call, ready for a 7.30 a.m. departure. He was pleasantly surprised when, answering the knock on the door next morning, he found a waiter bearing a heavily laden tray, none of which he had ordered.

'Morning sir,' said the waiter deferentially. 'Please have this full Irish breakfast, compliments of the manager. There's a full set of English and Irish newspapers, compliments of the manager. Half a bottle of finest French champagne, compliments of the manager. Oh yes, and a jug of freshly squeezed orange juice.'

'Why?' asked the puzzled but delighted Belgian. 'I didn't order any of these things.'

'Well, sir,' said the waiter, backing off. 'It could have something to do with the fact that it has just turned nine o'clock.'

● At the UEFA Cup tie between Bohemians and Aberdeen, played in the Republic, the announcer was clearly delighted to make a very important announcement over the tannoy. 'It is my great pleasure to tell you tonight that our mascot, Paddy, is back. As many of you will know, he suffered a terrible head injury recently, but I am happy to say he is fully recovered and is with us today. I want you to put your hands together and give Paddy an extra big hand.'

On the signal the gate was opened and out raced a black labrador, over the line, across the pitch, past the startled captains who were waiting to toss up, over the other side of the pitch and head first into the advertising hoardings, to the plaintive cry over the loudspeaker: 'Jesus – he's done it again!'

● At the same game the Aberdeen players were surprised by a discreet knock on their door during the half-time break.

'Just to let you know, sir,' said the man at the door, 'we will be playing in the same colours in the second half as we played in the first.'

Pancho

● Manchester United and England centre forward Stuart Pearson was quite often on the wrong end of Tommy Docherty's biting wit, especially over the unfortunate string of injuries that prematurely finished his career. After Doc had left Old Trafford, returning as manager of Derby County, he immediately sought out 'Pancho' to wind him up with the enquiry: 'Found any new ways of getting injured?'

Pearson shrugged off the remark so well that within five minutes of the kick-off he'd scored United's opening goal. Then, turning to the Stretford End, he gave his familiar stiff-armed salute . . . only to tear a muscle in his arm and be led away for treatment, to the inevitable mirth of the wicked Doc.

New Boy

● Another footballer who used a similar technique was Arsenal goalkeeper John Lukic. When he was at Leeds, if a team announcement included a new boy, he'd nip out to a telephone, ring the club and, taking off a national newspaper reporter's voice, he'd conduct a long interview, which he taped and then played back to the poor player, in front of all his mocking teammates.

Media Madness

● Journalists are often told – without any effect – to write tight. Eric Todd of *The Guardian* showed the perfect economy of words in his match report on a goalless draw between Bradford City and Barnsley.

He wrote: 'And they say footballers are under-paid.'

• The popular *Mail on Sunday* reporter, Bob Cass, wishes he had been as circumspect when he dabbled in local radio in the formative days of that medium. The local Geordie station was flashing around the local grounds, picking up late team news and increasingly bad reports of the weather with the link man saying, 'And now over to St James' Park and Bob Cass. What's the weather like with you, Bob?'

'Aye, its f————ng pissing down here.'

• On another occasion Bob was helping out one of the heavy Sunday papers before moving on to the *Mail*. When asked to write a piece of 800 words he replied that he didn't know 800 words.

• BRMB, the local Birmingham station, like most, slot in little after-match interviews with their heroes, and often the sequence is upset as their reporters scurry around dressing-rooms trying to persuade someone to come and speak to them. Harry Llewellyn was particularly pleased to be able to tell the studio that he had the charismatic West Bromwich Albion goalkeeper, John Osborne, waiting to talk to the listening Midlands. Eventually the studio got round to the Baggies game, linking in their man on the spot: 'And now over to Harry Llewellyn who has Albion goalkeeper John Osborne with him . . . Harry.'

Back came the immortal reply, live on air: 'He's buggered off, Tony.'

• Gordon Lee was commentating on the 1978 World Cup when he came out with the classic, 'It's difficult enough for the English teams like Wales, let alone the European teams like Brazil.'

• Writers can usually rely on their offices to pick up their howlers, but there is no such back-up for the electronic media men. Another who has earned fame around the circuit for his howlers is Glasgow radio man David Francie. He became a legend in his own lunchtime when reporting the Scotland versus Zaire game in Dortmund during the World Cup in West Germany in 1974. His build-up would have done Barbara Cartland credit with descriptions of the weather, the stadium and every detail of every Scots player, painting a perfect picture for his listeners – until the opposition ran out to the unforgivable comment: 'And here come the darkies.' What a good job I wasn't the one who said it!

• These boys don't have a lot of time to think and often rely on a colleague feeding them bits they've missed, causing the inevitable clangers. One of the venerable BBC men once baffled his listeners by saying, for no apparent reason, 'And don't forget to mention the band.' So no wonder poor David Francie had problems when the studio went over to him moments after the start of a European Cup game between Rangers and Red Star Belgrade at Ibrox.

'Tragedy, tragedy, tragedy,' he began, with his usual gift for understatement. 'Rangers are already one down, and what a great goal it was with the ball worked down the right, crossed into the middle for the big number nine, the strapping Yugoslav, the Red Star international ...', desperately playing for time while nudging his colleague for the name of the goalscorer. A piece of paper was slipped in front of him and he confidently continued '... scored by Buggered If I Know.'

● The south Americans got it right. They just howled 'Gooooooooooooooo-oooooooooooooooooooooooooooal. Gol, gol, gol, gooooal' until someone came up with the name. Not Francie.

'Unforgettable goal,' he enthused into the mike. 'Wee Willie Johnstone took them all on, beat the entire defence and crossed to the far post where ... where ... where ... where someone headed an unforgettable goal.'

● *Daily Telegraph* reporter Colin Gibson was on his way to the airport by taxi after a game in Dublin when the driver put on a particularly attractive tape.

'What's that piece of music?' asked Colin, genuinely interested, only to be told, 'I don't know, I only work Thursdays.'

● But sometimes it is the journalists who get sent up. A group of Millwall supporters with a wicked sense of humour hatched up a story during the week before a third-round Cup tie against Arsenal at Highbury. They telephoned a particular journalist on the *Daily Mirror* with the news that they planned to steal the famous, huge clock at the visitors' end of the ground. Not only did the journalist buy the story, so did his sports editor, and the paper ran a lurid story of the 'Millwall Plot'. It needed only a little thought to realise that to remove a piece of metal that size the supporters would have to smuggle welding equipment and heavy lifting gear past the 500 police on duty. For once the voices of the two rival London clubs were in unison in their chants of derision aimed at the unfortunate journalist.

● My co-author, Bob Harris, was the victim of one of the best-ever cons while in Belgrade for an England game against Yugoslavia. Always a bit of a flashy dresser, Bob emerged on the terrace to join his colleagues, resplendent in a white suit that reflected the close-season atmosphere. He sat down and ordered a very dry vodka martini on the rocks only to be given a tiny glass of beer by the waiter. Not a beer drinker at the best of times, Bob raved at the gormless waiter and repeated his order, only to be brought yet another small beer.

In exasperation Bob stormed out and made for one of the other bars in the big Hotel Jugoslavia. Again the order went in and again back came a beer. The same thing happened in the next bar, and the next, until Bob saw the grinning face of Frank McGhee, now of *The Observer*, who had collared the hotel manager and told him that he was the lawyer for the alcoholic son of an eccentric billionaire, and whatever drink was ordered they were only to give him a beer.

● In Cyprus Bob unintentionally sent himself up when he came down the marble staircase dressed in his white suit, only to walk into a large group of men all wearing white suits. A discreet enquiry revealed that it was traditional costume for a local wedding, with the reception being held at the hotel. Exit Bob to change his clothes.

• Another own goal was scored by the Italian journalists who unanimously wrote off their team's chances before the 1982 World Cup Finals in Spain. The Italians went on to win and the writers were pelted with rotten fruit when they returned home.

• Ian Botham's long charity walk in Ireland coincided with an England World Cup qualifier against Northern Ireland, and a number of the football writers were asked by their offices to cover the Press conference, which was to be held at 6 p.m. in a pub conveniently close to their hotel. It was so close that the boys were there some ten to fifteen minutes before opening time, but when they knocked on the door the barman answered, 'We don't open until six o'clock, but come in and have a drink while you are waiting.' Now that's true Irish hospitality!

Practice Makes Perfect

• Football crowds are also a good source of laconic humour – and not just in Liverpool either. Cockney humour can often match the Scouser jibe for jibe. Play was halted for an injury in a particularly tepid local derby between Chelsea and Fulham when a plaintive voice called out: 'For God's sake don't just stand there – *practice*!' Later,

when another player went down – injured or plain tired – another voice chirped up: 'Don't stop the game ref – he'll tread in eventually.'

Early Closing

• When Dave Mackay was trying to sign Gerry Daly for Derby County from Manchester United, the deal amost fell through because of a lack of local knowledge on the player's part and a failure by the manager to appreciate a player's thinking. Mackay told Daly he would meet him at 1 p.m. in the 'Midland' – at that time the hub of all Midlands football. Mackay, an imposing figure whether in football kit or civvies, was not a man to be taken lightly and he was surprised, to put it mildly, when one o'clock came and went with no Daly. So did 2.00, 2.30, 3.00, until a disgusted Mackay angrily left the Midland Hotel, only to find a frustrated Gerry Daly shuffling his feet outside the Midland Bank.

CHAPTER
5

That Old Mushe Mshonga

An Africa witch-doctors are a part of everyday life – and that includes football as well! No self-respecting team would be without their magic man, and even the Zimbabwe national team took a juju with them to Egypt for a World Cup qualifying match. When we lost by only a single goal in a game where we were expected to be thrashed, the credit went to him rather than to me.

It is not something even a white man takes lightly and, indeed, it has been pointed out to me that since I wrote about the dudus (the top magic men), the jujus (the ordinary medicine men) and their Mushe Mshonga (strong magic) in my autobiography, I have suffered many more injuries and missed many more games than before. It conjures up images of partly naked witch-doctors, with bones through their noses, sitting in a grass hut in the middle of a jungle and sticking pins into various parts of a Bruce Grobbelaar *Spitting Image* doll.

But true or not, I know that the two holes in my right leg were caused by my own team-mate, Steve McMahon, going over the top to me in a typically tough Liverpool practice match. I don't know whether he is in cahoots with any juju men, but if he is, perhaps he should speak to them about an aura of protection for himself.

Although I can't see Bobby Robson bringing in a magic man to throw the bones before an England international, or Kenny Dalglish burning a bonfire of hashish in the Liverpool dressing-room before games, you can be sure that as long as witchcraft, magic, call it what you will, is practised in Africa or the West Indies or South America, it will be exported to the most civilised of countries. And since I have been playing for Liverpool, I have stumbled across some strange goings-on, even at Anfield.

Let's face it, the witch-doctor is only the equivalent of a Western homeo-pathic or herbal doctor, or a prac-titioner of acupuncture in the Orient and a Medicine Man in North America. All over the world there is a natural form of medicine which has developed through the ages. Maybe in Africa they

You can Count on one hand the number of goalkeepers who like crosses

embellish it just a little for effect. Witch-doctors are certainly recognised in my old homeland of Zimbabwe, and when Rhodesia became independent they were given the title of 'doctor', which gave them considerable respectability. In fact, there are many who believe they played a huge part in gaining that independence.

From personal experience I have known people cured of asthmatic illnesses and the like with the use of herbal medicine. I have also seen the bad effects and the other side of the practice, particularly in the jungle where the influence of the juju and dudu has been all-powerful. There the immense power of suggestion has been enough to hypnotise an ill-educated man or women into doing something beyond the imagination of a normal person. In these outposts the witch-doctor was everything: medicine man, agony aunt, judge and jury. Tribesmen would even take their marital problems to the juju, whose solution would often be somewhat more terminal than divorce!

In the dark ages these dudus, looked up to by the lesser jujus, wielded so much power that if they told their Matabele chief that the only route to salvation was to go and kill a hundred 'Shona Dogs', off the village braves would go to do exactly that! The same beliefs are still deeply engrained in the tribes, though nowadays the witch-doctors are a little more modern and tend to play second fiddle to the powerful politicians, who in turn still have their own personal dudus whom they consult before making major decisions.

Things have changed. The bones they throw nowadays are the knuckles of goats and pigs rather than of humans, and they tend to wear designer sports shirts and slacks rather than skirts made of the tails of goats or, more powerful, monkeys. There are no bones through noses, to destroy another white man's concept, and while a big dudu may wear a monkey skin as a head-dress for a bit of serious Mushe Mshonga, more often than not you can only identify them by their less obvious adornments.

The leather thong around the wrist, ankle or neck is often a real giveaway, as is the goat's tail carried like a riding crop. There are a few notable African doctors, well known politically throughout the world, who not only carry the title of doctor but also the goat's-tail switch – and it isn't for flicking away the flies!

Every magic man I have known or been involved with through football has carried his goat's tail to dip into his own secret potion: not so much tail of bat, eye of spider and larynx of ant-eater, as grass, seeds, oil, herbs, blood of an ox, hair from a goat's tail and goats' urine. I was always getting the foul stuff splashed over me when I was playing football in Africa, even for the national team.

It wasn't so bad in Egypt, because we went through the rituals in the comfort of a five-star luxury hotel on the banks of the Nile. The Zimbabwe coach actually got permission from the Zimbabwe Football Association to take his own dudu with us – ticket and expenses paid for. They might have a magic sponge in England, but we had real magic in Egypt! He gave us each a portion of potion to pop in our bath water, but judging by the smell I don't think it would ever catch on in the Hilton chain of hotels.

We weren't allowed to dry ourselves after the bath, but all trotted up the corridor in our bath towels to the witch-doctor's room, where we shed our towels and 18 of us stood in a cramped circle, stark naked, with this magic man walking around the outside of the circle flicking at us with his goat's tail. We had to put our kit on before the stuff dried.

Worse still, he wanted me to spread some foul smelling grease on my gloves. Can you imagine that? As if I don't have enough trouble holding on to the ball without some clown trying to make it even more difficult! I couldn't talk my way out of that one, and the 1−0 result was a great one, even if it did go against us.

Suspicion and superstition rule supreme in all African football – but then doesn't it everywhere? How often do you hear of an English manager with a lucky suit or a lucky tie, a player who puts his kit on in a certain order (I do), or the left boot before the right boot, or even running out in a special order?

However, thankfully they do not carry it quite as far as they did in South Africa or Zimbabwe. Can you imagine the Liverpool team changing into their playing kit in the Manchester United car park before a big game and refusing to use the dressing-room? Laughable, you'd think. Yet I rarely saw the inside of a dressing-room when I played my football in Africa, and I never went in goal for a warm-up before the kick-off, in case the ball went in the net and disturbed the juju's magic. That way of thinking was so engrained that I carried on the practice (or not) when I played for a while with Crewe Alexandra in the Fourth Division of the Football League! The idea was that the witch-doctor would build barriers before the kick-off, and if the ball passed through they would have been broken.

We were banned from the dressing-rooms, particularly at away grounds, because the opposition's witch-doctor might have stronger magic. I have changed into my goalkeeper's gear in school rooms, buses, car parks, on hills overlooking the stadium and with gawping, giggling girls watching to catch a glimpse of the difference between black and white men. One of the strangest changing-rooms I used was in the Risco Steel mines. I have even climbed, with the rest of my team, a six-foot-high fence around the pitch, simply to avoid entering the dressing-room or running down the tunnel.

Over the years I have become expert at changing my clothes in public without showing enough to be arrested for indecent exposure. I would be a revelation – or not – changing under a hand-towel on a British beach.

My first experience of the connection between football and witch-craft was in South Africa, when an English-born goalkeeper named Peter B'alac played for Lusitano. Like all Europeans, he ignored the rites and rituals but without offending anyone. This attitude backfired when the team juju gave him a little lock and chain to put in the back of his net before an important Cup tie. He wasn't too keen on getting involved, but threw it down before the kick-off and then forgot all about it as he stood back, playing little more than a spectator's role while his team pressed forward.

It was only at half time, when the witch-doctor asked him what he had done with the charm, that he remembered he had left it where it had been dropped. The desperate witch-doctor flew out, but his rival had beaten him to it and the lock and chain had vanished. The juju was distraught, but Peter simply shrugged and decided to go out and show these ignorant people that he did not believe in their superstitions. A fair bet, as his team-mates had been so much on top in the first half.

They retained their domination, but simply could not score as the opposition goalkeeper turned in a world-class performance, aided and abetted by the woodwork and goal-line clearances from his fellow defenders. They rarely broke out of their own half – only six times in fact – but they scored on each breakaway, with the shots whistling from every angle, past the surprised Englishman.

Witch-doctor 1 Peter B'alac 0!

There was an odd sequel to this story some years later in England when Gary Bailey, an old South African opponent of mine, playing for Manchester United in an FA Cup Final against Brighton, was given a little locket tied with the red and white of his team as a gift from some South African friends. Gary, like most Europeans in Africa, had heard the B'alac story and, though an intelligent, educated man, he took no chances and carried the charm with him. Having conceded two goals in the first drawn game, Gary kept a clean sheet in a 4–0 win.

On his next visit to Wembley, in his first full game for England, he conceded an embarrassingly soft goal near the end. Needless to say when he returned for another FA Cup Final appearance for Manchester United against the strong favourites, Everton, he was determined that there would be a lock and chain in his goal-mouth. The whole of Britain got to know about African superstitions when Gary left the talisman behind in Manchester, and a major operation was required to arrange for it to be with him when he trotted out.

Everton, who had already won the League Championship and the European Cup-Winners' Cup, could not beat Bailey. Even when United had Kevin Moran sent off there was still no way past, and United, against all the odds, won 1–0.

Gary's bright career in England was eventually ended by a severe training injury sustained with England before the Mexico World Cup. It was so bad that, despite operations and the best medical care money could buy, Gary was forced to quit and return home to South Africa. Within a couple of years he was back playing for Kaiser Chiefs. He swears it was top surgeons and medical men in South Africa who worked this miracle cure . . . but I just wonder if there was any Mushe Mshonga involved!

We non-believers are supposed to be above it all, but when you brush shoulders with it, some must rub off and you cannot dismiss it completely. I saw too many incidents that defied natural explanation to ignore it.

I thought I had witnessed the death of one of these dudus once, not yards away from me when he got one of his mates to drive a lance through his body. I believed the trick had misfired when I saw the blood spurt as the spear went in one side and out of the other. There was nothing fake about that. But this black Paul Daniels simply pulled out the spear, jumped to his feet, did a little war dance, and the exhibition was over. Maybe it was a show of strength to the white army boys, but I was so staggered by what I had seen that I went back a couple of days later to check the guy out. He was still alive and kicking, with a scab on each side of his body where the spear had gone in and out.

Nothing much has changed since I was over there, for in February 1988 Robert Mugabe sent three young Air Force footballers to Liverpool to train and study our methods. Needless to say I was lumbered – I mean asked – to keep an eye on them while they were on Merseyside. They were telling me how the Air Force team had finished seventh, seventh and fifth in successive seasons since their promotion to the top Division, but could not make that final step forward to be among the honours. The three boys were convinced that the fault lay with their juju, who also worked for the top team, the Black Rhinos of the Armed Forces whose Commander-in-Chief is none other than Prime Minister Robert Mugabe, alias Minister of Defence.

Whenever these two rival teams meet, the Rhinos always win by the odd goal, and although they are totally convinced that he gives the stronger magic to the Rhinos, no one in the Air Force team is strong enough to fire him and bring in outside help. Mind you that is not always the case, for while the witch-doctors are always ready to take the credit for victory, the supporters will often blame him rather than the players in an important defeat.

I could have stayed a true infidel through one of my earliest experiences with a magic man back in Rhodesia, when I was playing for Salisbury Callies against Chibuku one Sunday. On Friday their witch-doctor turned up at our ground, resplendent in goat's-tail skirt and monkey head-dress, waving his goat's tail and carrying his bucket of herbs and other bits. We did everything we could to chase him away, even to the extent of putting him in a car and driving him five miles back to his township. Within a few hours he was back throwing his bones in each of the goal-mouths, running up and down the pitch and making a real pest of himself. But it was certainly ten out of ten for effort and application and, in the end, we let him get on with it.

On the match day he was the busiest man on the pitch, up and down the touchline like an extra linesman but, despite his efforts. Callies won 3–2 after extra time, and we last saw him being chased up the road by irate, stone-throwing Chibuku fans.

By the time I had switched from the all-white Callies to the almost all-black Chibuku, they had a new magic-man, and before we clashed with Callies he gave me a little bone to roll into my sock when I got changed. At half time we were two down and the witch-doctor, seeing my socks around my ankles, asked me where the bone was. It had fallen out, and I had not even noticed. He was furious, handing me another bone with the threat: 'Bruce – if we lose this game I would not be in your shoes.'

Now this was really going to put the old voodoo to the test, and I wasn't too keen on being the guinea pig. To make matters worse, the duiker bone, which I had put down my sock, had worked its way into my boot, acting as an uncomfortable reminder of the threat hanging over my head. Fortunately, we scraped through 3–2, but after that Billy Sharman, Nimo Schilacki and I

Often, keeping goal behind a defence as good as Liverpool's means hanging around waiting for the occasional cross

made a stand against the influence this man was wielding. Assistant manager John Garatsa fought against it, and although some of the blacks were 'sore afraid' when we eventually booted him out, it was all soon forgotten after we put together a long winning run without the help of bones or monkey tails.

South Africa worked on exactly the same principles, although the witch-doctors were perhaps a little more up-to-date, with the skirt of tails worn over modern boxer shorts. When I played for AmaZulu, ours would come to our training sessions on a bit of waste ground behind Smugglers' Inn. He would make us stand in a circle and then flick his goat's tail at our knees, repeating the ritual after the session, while we waited impatiently to nip off for a well-earned beer and a look at the strippers in the local pub.

It seems to me that a great deal of the magic revolved around drugs. You can't disguise that sickly, sweet smell — as I discovered only too well in my army days. Often you couldn't see out of the bus windows because of the billowing clouds of smoke, and in both South Africa and Rhodesia quite often the players would gather in a group around a smoking pile of leaves, sometimes with dung mixed in to disguise the fact that the burning leaves were, in fact, marijuana. In some of the big cities, though, the officials weren't too keen on the practice of little, smelly bonfires in their dressing-rooms and corridors.

Once, when playing Maritzburg at the Kingsmead Stadium, they were so fed up with our juju that they tried to ban him. No way. My black team-mates threw a wobbly and refused to play unless he was allowed in the dressing-rooms. For the sake of the spectators they relented ten minutes before the kick-off, which was then delayed while the smug magic-man threw his bones and went through his business.

The surprising factor was that our coach was a down-to-earth Irishman, Harry Weir, who had to stand back and let all this happen, including the little bonfires. When I asked him why, he shrugged and said, 'How can an Irishman tell an African what to do in Africa? I just have to follow what they do.'

The exasperated officials at the Rand Stadium in Johannesburg finally burst into the dressing-room as our man waved his tail, chanted his words and tried to kindle a little fire in the corner. He was instantly ordered to put it out by the Fire Chief, who claimed it was a fire hazard. Undaunted, he crushed a few of the smouldering leaves in his hand and had my team-mates sniff the smoke as they trotted out for what everyone was predicting would be a massacre in favour of the white team. We drew 1–1 and scored a victory for the Zulu nation against a team of ten white men and one token black. It was a moral victory, an outstanding performance by every player. But who got the credit? You've guessed it — the witch-doctor!

The scary thing was that he had predicted before the game that one of the officials would be injured — and sure enough a linesman was knocked unconscious by a thrown brick after flagging for offside when the home side scored. He was injured badly enough to be replaced.

I've experienced these predictions before. In the army one of the jujus used to throw the bones before we went out on patrol to tell us whether we should take our tents in case of rain, because no one wanted to carry overweight luggage, but nor did we want to get soaked in a monsoon. They were about as accurate as Michael Fish on hurricanes; on one trip the rain came a day early and we all got soaked, and a forecast ambush came two days late and we almost got killed.

But I never mocked the medicine man and his Mshonga too much, for there is no doubt that some of those herbs did cure, and the power of suggestion will always be a potent weapon for good or evil. Don't Western doctors use sugar pills and even hypnosis? Witch-craft in any other language.

More often than not those involved in sport were jujus rather than dudus. Sport was considered a little too frivolous for the top men, who were concerned with the weightier matters of politics in the big cities and with the tribal chiefs in the outback. Occasionally the big men became involved if there was a major political or national victory to be gained, such as in the Olympic Games.

Before the 1980 Games in Moscow, the Soviets, under threat of a major boycott over the invasion of Afghanistan, hustled around the world trying to persuade as many friends as they could to make up the numbers. They made a particular effort in Africa, asking them to send as many competitors as possible and promising that the Kremlin would pick up the tab, pay all expenses and even fly them to Moscow. It was an offer that could not be refused, and among the eager volunteers was an all-white team of lady hockey players, a motley crew including the youngest Olympic hockey player, teenager Arlene Boxhall, and the oldest female, 35-year-old player-coach Anthea Stewart.

Naturally enough, our newly independent nation wanted to acquit themselves well under the world spotlight, so they called in a top dudu to assist these white ladies before they left for the Soviet Union. I am not sure it was strictly within the letter of the Olympic ideals, but I can exclusively reveal that they were offered a bribe in the unlikely event of their winning. The prize was to be a mombi (a cow) and a street in their own area named after each player.

With this promise ringing in their ears, and the bones predicting triumph on Moscow soil – or grass – they set off in three ancient Rhodesian Air Force Dakotas to Lusaka, where they were picked up by a Soviet Ilyushin.

What followed is history. The team, which had hardly ever played together, produced one of the greatest Olympic shocks of all time, the hosts being relegated to third place while Zimbabwe beat the Czechs to win the first-ever women's Olympic hockey gold medal. No doubt the witch-doctor, who had not travelled with them, took all the credit, but by the time the

team got back a party had been arranged to celebrate their glorious achievement. There they were ceremoniously presented with their promised bonus, but instead of a cow each they had a couple shared between them in the form of a Braai Ulies pack, consisting of a piece of rump, fillet and sirloin, a T-bone, beef sausages and liver. What's more, they were expected to open their prizes at the barbecue.

Although the jujus would also involve themselves in boxing and athletics when it suited their purposes to impress, it was football that mostly attracted them because of its big following.

Goalkeepers were, for obvious reasons, especially susceptible to any mumbo jumbo doing the rounds. If there is a player in the team who can affect a result single-handedly it is the poor old goalie. A brilliant save or an horrendous boob can change the course of a match in an instant – and therein lay a strange tale concerning the experienced Arcadia goalkeeper, Stuart Gilbert. This was no impressionable kid; this was the man who performed wonders for his country in the World Cup play-offs in Australia in 1969. He told the story himself that when he was playing against Mangula Mines, the ball turned into a roaring lion's head whenever it came towards him – and he conceded six goals.

This was undoubtedly the influence of the heavy, heady narcotics used by the witch-doctors rather than any serious magic, yet in a way I suppose the effects were magic. In the same way there can be no other explanation for the way the Matabele Highlanders cen-

tre half played on with a leg broken in two places. Zenzo 'Elephant' Ndlovu was only 5ft 8in tall, but he smoked so much grass that he had no trouble outjumping the biggest of centre forwards, even if it meant landing on his backside after every jump. This man actually played on with his leg broken in two places, collapsing only as he came off the pitch. What is more, he was back playing in nine weeks. Another Zimbabwe international, Oliver Kataya, was nicknamed 'Flying Saucer' because he was always so high on the weed.

But neither hash nor any other narcotic could account for the cure of Matabele Highlanders goalkeeper Peter Nkomo who, when I was with the club, played for the Under-12 team. What made him stand out in the memory was that he always kept goal with his permanently stiff left leg bandaged from thigh to ankle. There was something seriously wrong and yet, without having visited a surgeon, he suddenly appeared without the bandage or the limp, and went on to make the national squad.

It is all too easy to sneer at something you don't understand. But once you have been exposed to it, there is no doubt at all that even the most hardened non-believer becomes wary, if not aware. Old films and fables build up something of a myth in the West, although there are now no bones through the noses and most of the top dudus in the city will have a wardrobe of fine clothes, wearing the monkey tails over modern underwear to protect their dignity. More often than not the top men will be entitled to use the word doctor before their name, wear city suits and let it be known that they are what they are only by a discreet leather wristlet and the inevitable swish stick. They move in only the best company and even now, I am told, every six weeks or so Robert Mugabe is presented with a small long-tailed rodent called a pankalen.

Apparently, the significance is that the pankalen was scarcely seen before independence, and legend now has it that this animal, a little like a spring hare or a small kangaroo, was used by the big dudus in gaining the country's freedom. In the past they were presented to the big tribal chiefs. God knows what Mr Mugabe does with the eight or nine he receives every year — perhaps he just releases the creature, and it is the same one coming back each time. That's quite possible, as they are a protected species. Not that they need much protection if they are under the close control of the men who make the Mushe Mshonga!

At the Hotel Victoria near where I live in Heswall, the local punters firmly believe that I practise the black arts myself — not because of any supernatural goalkeeping skills, but for my crystal ball-gazing powers. Their favourite team, Everton, were playing Arsenal at Goodison Park in the first leg of the semi-final of the Littlewoods Cup, and the game was being televised live on a Sunday afternoon. Before the game the conversation had turned to witch-doctors and, with no goat's-knuckle bones to throw, I used a few beer bottle caps to predict that Arsenal would win 1–0.

Amazingly, Arsenal, who had been struggling for some weeks in the League, made full use of a gale force wind at their backs to lay siege to the home goal. In fact, they were unlucky to go in at half time with only a spectacular goal from Perry Groves to show for their superiority. The Everton supporters in the bar were surprised, but confident that my prediction would come well and truly unstuck when Everton enjoyed the wind behind them, especially after Tony Adams conceded a penalty for climbing all over Graeme Sharpe. I threw some more caps and told them that Trevor Steven would miss. He did, and what is more, Arsenal held on until the end to make my forecast come true. So I am now looked upon with new respect on the Wirral, where I am known as the local juju man, the Wirral Witch-doctor.

Don't mock! It happens all over the civilised world, but some countries prefer to call it religion rather than magic. The Italian team, Pescara, called in a monk to pray for deliverance from my former Liverpool team-mate Ian Rush who, despite an awful start with Juventus, couldn't help scoring against this one team. Of the first nine goals Rushy scored in Italy, seven of them came against Pescara, four in one game and three spread over another two games. The monk's Mushe Mshonga must have been strong, for not only did Rushy fail to score but Pescara upset all the odds by winning with a two-goal margin.

Nearer to home, the Liverpool players have become used to a man who would love to become the first official witch-doctor of an English League club. Fat chance he's got; it's taken them a century to get round to thinking of physiotherapists. His name is Humphs Junior, son of a Nigerian chief of some sort who was also a dudu. Humphs was born in the United States, but far from allowing that to hold him back, he plunged headlong into spiritualism while studying law and psychiatry. He gained a little credibility in the players' bar when we had a good run and he successfully predicted a few correct scores, including an Ian Rush hat-trick. He had his powder of crushed skull, beetle dung and whatever substance that I put on to humour him, but it became a bit much when I kept a clean sheet and he claimed the credit. Not just the credit either. He wanted to be rewarded with match tickets and even a few five pound notes – usually because his allowance had been delayed. Typical African, black or white – like a sponge – squeeze and vanish.

But, of course, the effect of the magic can never be quite the same anywhere else as it is under a starry sky in Africa. Scotty Road has to be different from the Honde Valley; the effect has to be different. For a start, the heavy lorries would drown out the witch-doctors' means of communication. No, not drums. They didn't need them. Their transmission messages to the gods and to each other are spectacular to say the least. I have heard their messages go up to a relay station 1,500 feet up from the Honde Valley floor as the sing-song chants are picked up by one juju and passed on to another. With the wind in the right direction you can stand in one spot and hear it go east to west like listening to some sophisticated hi-fi stereophonic recording.

A bit like the Kop in full voice, really. They have a magic all of their own.

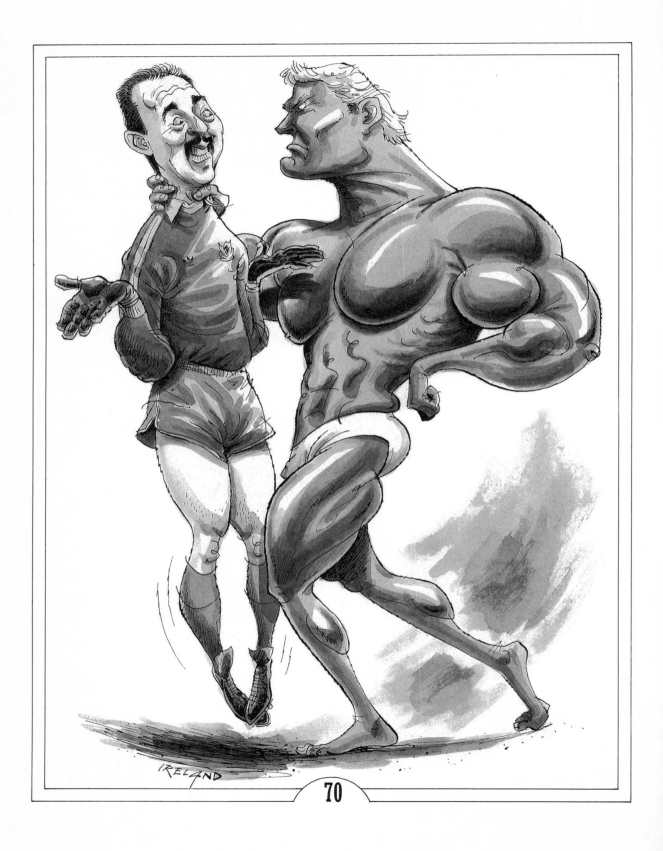

Lists

Every footballer builds his life around lists — notably the one that appears in the dressing-room before a game. It's the best feeling in the world when you're on it, but maybe some players will change their mind when they read mine. Sorry chaps!

Gamesmanship

1. My old team-mate Graeme Souness pulled one of the best flankers ever against the Russian champions, Dynamo Kiev, in the European Cup—and got away with it. Manager of Glasgow Rangers, he was worried about his defence against the speedy breaks of his rivals. So, after letting Dynamo train on the big Ibrox pitch, he had his groundsman reduce the width by several feet each side. Rangers won and the Russians were so furious they lodged an official complaint to the UEFA representative, who was forced to take a tape measure out after the game to prove it was six inches within the regulations.

2. The day Luton Town went missing. Luton undoubtedly shattered the rules of the FA Cup when, with Liverpool's pitch perfectly playable and Luton fans and even directors making their way to Merseyside, the team left their flight to Speke Airport too late and had to cry off. Under any other Cup rules, Liverpool should have been awarded the tie. To make matters worse, Luton drew when they eventually turned up, and then beat us on their awful plastic pitch, making our moans sound like sour grapes.

3. Not strictly gamesmanship, but the way it worked out the sewer collapse under the Kop at Anfield helped Liverpool to a flying start in their record-breaking League Centenary season.

4. Artificial turf — whether it is at Luton, Preston, QPR, Oldham or anywhere else — gives an unfair advantage to the home team and has still to prove conducive to good football.

5. Witch-doctors. Now if that's not gamesmanship then I don't know what is. Fortunately, it has never caught on over here, although in the First Division former Manchester United goalkeeper Gary Bailey and I have both dabbled in it gently. But to some Africans it was the difference between playing well and playing badly; between winning and losing.

6. Liverpool in Russia. No wonder Souness was so keen to stitch up the Russians after supporters of Dynamo Tbilisi, escorted by police, went on a torchlight parade around the team hotel at 3 a.m., waking up every player the night before an European Cup tie. Liverpool lost.

7. Maradona's hand ball. The only way Diego Maradona could have outjumped Peter Shilton to put Argentina into the lead against England in the quarter-finals of the World Cup in Mexico City was to have used his hand. Television quickly proved the theory, but the officiating was so weak, particularly from the linesman, that the goal was given and the game turned in favour of the South Americans, who went on to win the World Cup.

8. Our former manager, Bob Paisley, had a variety of ways of getting important tactical messages to players during the course of a match, but the classic bit of gamesmanship by this shrewd Geordie was when a terrier ran on to the

You need hands

pitch during an FA Cup tie. The crowd, and even the referee, enjoyed the sight of Bob chasing the dog around the pitch, little knowing that he was passing on hints to two or three of the players.

9. Who's counting? If the witch-doctors don't work, then try cheating. At least that's what Accra Great Olympic Football Club of Ghana tried when they found themselves, not unexpectedly, trailing to the Brazilian team Palmeiras. They slipped a couple of substitutes on to the pitch . . . without taking anyone off.

10. That wasn't a heavy tackle that was my brother. The strikingly similar Forster brothers almost pulled off one of the greatest cons in football in a Bundesliga match in West Germany. Karl-Heinz had already been cautioned by the referee when he committed another bookable offence. In stepped brother Bernd to assure the confused official that it was he who had had his

name taken in the first place. They would have got away with it as well had they kept quiet and not boasted to the newspapers. Both were punished.

11. Celtic v Rapid Vienna. UEFA have made many strange decisions but none more so than when they supported the most blatant piece of gamesmanship in the history of the game by upholding a crazy Austrian appeal. Having already rejected a ludicrous claim that Weinhofer had been hit by a bottle thrown from the crowd – when television and every witness in the stadium saw it land yards from him – on the evidence of their own observer and the referee they overturned it on appeal and ordered the game to be replayed at Manchester United's ground. So detailed was the con that the player left the ground with his head bandaged. Celtic had overcome a 3–1 deficit to win 3–0 at home, but in the replayed game lost 1–0 when the goalscorer and goalkeeper were assaulted by fans.

Sports That Turn Me Off

1. Synchronised swimming (Drowning in style).
2. Darts (Fat-bellied non-sportsmen).
3. Speedway (Mud in the eye).
4. Stock Car Racing (Waste of good machinery).
5. Pigeon Racing (One in the eye).
6. Speed Boat Racing (Pleasure not sport).
7. Three-day Eventing (Two days too long).
8. Archery (Like watching grass grow).
9. Mud Wrestling (Or wrestling of any sort).
10. Mr Universe (What happened to the drug tests?).
11. Carpet Bowls (Better things to do on carpets).

The Best of the Enemy

(In no particular order as long as they are not lining up to take shots at me!)

1. Ian Rush (Wales).
2. Gary Lineker (England).
3. Johann Cruyff (Holland).
4. Kenny Dalglish (Scotland).
5. Kevin Keegan (England).
6. George Best (Northern Ireland).
7. Pele (Brazil).
8. Eusebio (Portugal).
9. Bobby Charlton (England).
10. Gerd Müller (West Germany).
11. Ferenc Puskas (Hungary).
12. Jimmy Greaves (England).

A.K.A.

1. **Bruce Grobbelaar** – Jungle Man, Blue or Slap.
2. **Steve Nicol** – Chico or Chopsy.
3. **Gary Gillespie** – Dizzy or Stick.
4. **Alan Hansen** – Jocky.
5. **Steve McMahon** – Maca.
6. **Craig Johnston** – Roo, Kruggie or The Headless Chicken.
7. **John Barnes** – Digger or Tarmac.
8. **John Aldridge** – Aldo or Woody.
9. **Paul Walsh** – Ferret.
10. **Peter Beardsley** – Modo.
11. **Kevin MacDonald** – Albert.
12. **Kenny Dalglish** – Boss.
13. **Jimmy Beglin** – Dex.
14. **Ray Houghton** – Barney.
15. **Barry Venison** – Max.
16. **Ronnie Whelan** – Dusty.
17. **Ronnie Moran** – Bugsy.
18. **Jan Molby** – Danish Bacon.

John Motson's Nightmare Team

1. Eddie Niedzwiecki (Chelsea).
2. Reuben Agboola (Sunderland).
3. Wayne Cegielsk (Hereford).
4. Ricky Sbragia (York).
5. Romeo Zondervan (Ipswich).
6. John Gollogly (Hartlepool).
7. Andy Kowalski (Chesterfield).
8. Brian Scrimgeour (Chesterfield).
9. Marco Gabbiadini (Sunderland).
10. Chukwuemeka Nwajiobi (Luton).
11. Kenny Achampong (Fulham).

Subs: Aharon Fadida (Aldershot), Tarki Micallef (Barry Town), Joe Tortolano (Hibs), Michele Cecere (Oldham).

Grobbelaar's Greats

1. Lev Yachin (USSR).
2. Renate Dassaev (USSR).
3. Pat Jennings (Northern Ireland).
4. Peter Shilton (England).
5. Luis Arconada (Spain).
6. Dino Zoff (Italy).
7. Felix (Brazil).
8. Neville Southall (Wales).
9. Ray Clemence (England).
10. Jean-Marie Pfaff (Belgium).
11. Phil Parkes (England).
12. Gordon Banks (England).

Football League XI

1. Neville Southall (Everton).
2. Viv Anderson (Manchester United).
3. Steve Nicol (Liverpool).
4. Bryan Robson (Manchester United).
5. Mark Lawrenson (Liverpool).
6. Tony Adams (Arsenal).
7. Chris Waddle (Spurs).
8. Neil Webb (Nottingham Forest).
9. Peter Beardsley (Liverpool).
10. Graeme Sharp (Everton).
11. John Barnes (Liverpool).

Sub: Gary Mabbutt (Spurs).
Manager: Brian Clough.
Coaches: Bobby Robson, Ronnie Moran.

A Team Called Smith

1. Henry Smith (Hearts).
2. Brian Smith (Sheffield United).
3. Colin Smith (Aldershot).
4. Mark Smith (Sheffield Wednesday).
5. Mick Smith (Wimbledon).
6. Gary Smith (Fulham).
7. Bobby Smith (Leicester City).
8. Alan Smith (Arsenal).
9. Gordon Smith (Oldham).
10. Nigel P. Smith (Bristol City).
11. Nigel G. Smith (Stockport).

Chairman: John Smith (Liverpool).
Manager: Jim Smith (Oxford United).

A Team Not to Insult

(Just tip your hat politely – and leave by the nearest exit.)

1. John Burridge (Southampton).
2. Pat Van Den Hauwe (Everton).
3. Mark Dennis (QPR).
4. Graham Roberts (Chelsea).
5. Terry Butcher (Rangers).
6. Vinny Jones (Wimbledon).
7. Bryan Robson (Manchester United).
8. Norman Whiteside (Manchester United).
9. John Fashanu (Wimbledon).
10. Gary Thompson (Sheffield Wednesday).
11. Graeme Souness (Rangers).

Subs: Remi Moses (Manchester United), Joe Jordan (Bristol City), Steve Foster (Luton Town).

Bruce's Biggest Boobs

1. v CSKA Sofia, European Cup quarter-final. Liverpool, defending a slender one-goal lead from the first leg, found their game plan thrown into chaos when I called for a cross. I came tearing off my line and misjudged the ball completely to allow Mladenov to head one of Europe's softest goals, which set the Bulgarians on the way to a shock win.

2. v Widzew Lodz, a year later same competition, same stage, same result. This was when the story started that I cost Liverpool £250,000 from Vancouver Whitecaps – and £500,000 for two European Cups. On this occasion I slipped as I came off my line. I recovered in plenty of time but misjudged the pace of the centre and, instead of taking it in two hands, I tried to catch the ball one-handed. Not being blessed with Pat Jennings's big hands, I dropped the ball, which popped up for Tlokinski to tap home. P.S. I got the blame for the second, winning goal from Wraga as well!

3. v Sheffield Wednesday. The world – well, at least the British television viewers – rocked with mirth when Bruce, playing his sweeper's role, came racing yards out of his area to make an interception and pass the ball to the waiting Alan Kennedy. Instead it went straight to Imre Varadi, who stopped laughing long enough to sidefoot the ball past me and into the yawning net.

4. v Mutanga United FC. My début for Salisbury Callies in Rhodesia was wrecked when Sandy Crockart, my own centre half, nutmegged me for a spectacular own goal in a 3–1 defeat.

5. v AZ 67 Alkmaar. Another European Cup blunder, but this time with a happy ending. Having sacrificed a two-goal lead to draw 2–2 in Holland, we were cruising to a 2–1 home win when Johnny Metgod crossed a ball deep into our area. The scene looked like a pinball machine as the ball ricocheted be-

tween me, the back of Phil Thompson's head, the cross bar and, eventually, the net. Fortunately for me, a late Alan Hansen winner stole the headlines.

6. v Manchester City. A particularly unhappy Christmas for Bruce, when we lost 3–1 at home to Manchester City and Liverpool fans were more interested in my getting the sack – and not from Santa! Phil Thompson skied a ball in the air and my powder-puff punch let in little Asa Hartford for one of his rare goals.

7. v Manchester City. Same Boxing

Day disaster. Kevin Reeves whipped in a cross-shot, which I pushed on to the post. With me flapping, the ball rebounded, hit me on the head and went in. At least they couldn't blame me for Kevin Bond's penalty . . . or did they?

8. v Spurs. Even a friendly in the unlikely setting of Swaziland was not immune from Brucie's boobs when I threw the ball straight to Danny Thomas, who promptly volleyed the ball back past me from the halfway line.

9. v Witz University. Only my second game for Durban City in South Africa. Coach Roy Bailey had already dismissed me as hopeless when I found myself in direct opposition to his son, Gary, as we defended a long, unbeaten run. I tried to clear with my left foot, kicked it straight to the Witz centre forward and I had done it again. 'Bruce Boobs' said the headline – not a totally unusual one in the passing of the years.

10. v Oxford United. New manager Kenny Dalglish had been less than complimentary about my goalkeeping. His opinion did not improve when, with only minutes remaining, I came a long way off my line and was beaten by an Alan Kennedy back pass.

11. v Zambia. Playing in a vital African Cup match for Zimbabwe, I punched a centre rather too high in the air, and in a bid to recover it I followed the ball out of the area, only to collide with one of my own defenders as the ball squirted back into the net.

12. v Manchester United. Allowing myself to be conned into playing on against players like Norman Whiteside and Bryan Robson with a fractured elbow.

13. Watch this space!

Whoops!
(Or I'm not the only one who makes mistakes.)

1. 'I promise results, not promises.' John Bond.

2. 'Most of the things I have done are my own fault, so I can't feel guilty about them.' George Best.

3. '. . . and the crowd are encouraging referee Thomas to blow his watch.' Hugh Johns.

4. 'We're coming to the end of the half and the referee is looking at his whistle.' John Helm.

5. 'Thank you Jimmy Hill.' Russell Harty after interviewing Jimmy Greaves.

6. 'The Stoke City defender has a knee and thing injuries.' Who else but *The Guardian*?

7. 'The Austrians are wearing the dark black socks.' Barry Davies.

8. 'The King of Egypt's chief butler was not a bad man, but for some reason he had displeased this despotic monarch who promptly put him in goal.' *The Christian Herald.*

9. 'He placed the ball in the net and his delighted team-mates couldn't believe their lunch had finally changed.' *Liverpool Echo.*

10. 'As to general sanitary facilities, the stadium has 560 lavatories installed in private boxes and 1,526 located in places of easy access throughout the stadium. The stadium can be emptied completely in approximately eighteen minutes.' Blurb advertising the facilities at the Aztec Stadium in Mexico City.

11. '. . . and Forfar and Hamilton shared five goals.' Roddy Forsyth of BBC Radio, recording the first $2\frac{1}{2}$–$2\frac{1}{2}$ draw in living memory.

Baldies United

1. John Shaw (Exeter City).
2. David Armstrong (Bournemouth).
3. Derek Fazackerley (Bury).
4. Ray Wilkins (Rangers).
5. Terry Butcher (Rangers).
6. Johnny Metgod (Feyenoord).
7. Trevor Francis (QPR).
8. Cyrille Regis (Coventry City).
9. Derek Dawkins (Torquay United).
10. Steve McMahon (Liverpool).
11. Noel Brotherston (Bury).

Subs: Liam Brady (West Ham), Keith Cassells (Mansfield), Keith Walwyn (Blackpool), Alan Cook (Wimbledon), Bruce Grobbelaar (Liverpool).

Manager: Ron Atkinson.
Coach: Don Howe.
Assistant Coach: Terry Darracott.
Physiotherapist: Fred Street.
Press Officer: Bob Harris.

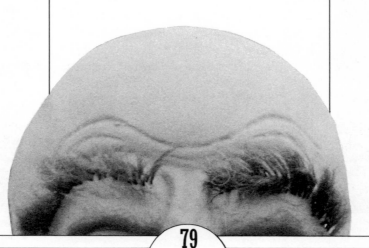

Over The Top

1. 'Trevor Brooking . . . he floats like a butterfly and stings like one too.' Brian Clough.

2. 'He's not so much a coach as a hearse.' Tommy Docherty.

3. 'There was a murderer on the pitch — the referee.' Uruguayan manager Omar Borras, after the referee had sent off one of his players after 40 seconds of a World Cup game against Scotland.

4. 'Beckenbauer is like Humpty Dumpty, and the team are playing like a bunch of cucumbers.' Third-choice West German goalkeeper, Uli Stein, during the Mexico World Cup. He was sent home.

5. 'If Graeme Souness was a chocolate drop he would eat himself.' Archie Gemmill during the Argentine World Cup.

6. 'Brian Clough is a kind of Rolls Royce Communist.' Malcolm Allison.

7. 'All this talk about Tommy Docherty not being fit to run a football club is rubbish. That's exactly what he is fit for.' Australian wit, broadcaster and author Clive James.

8. 'John Bond has blackened my name with his insinuations about the private lives of all football managers. Both my wives are upset.' Malcolm Allison.

9. 'The Manchester United manager . . . what's his name? You know, the Tank.' Publisher and football club collector Robert Maxwell, trying to recall the name of Manchester United's then manager, Ron Atkinson.

10. 'He's like a beautiful motor car is Duncan McKenzie. He's had six owners and been in the garage most of the time.' John Toshack.

11. 'Yes, I was the only one who was.' Sir Alf Ramsey's cutting response on being asked if he played for England in the 1950 World Cup Finals.

12. 'We have beaten England, England the home of the giants! Lord Nelson! Lord Beaverbrook! Sir Winston Churchill! Sir Anthony Eden! Clement Attlee! Henry Cooper! Lady Diana! Maggie Thatcher can you hear me – Maggie Thatcher I have a message for you in your campaigning. We have beaten England in the World Cup! As they say in your language, and as they say in the boxing bars around Madison Square Garden, your boys took one hell of a beating.' Norwegian TV commentator Bjorge Lillelien, after Norway had beaten England 2–1 in Oslo in 1981.

Team to Frighten the Children

1. Kenny Allen (Swindon Town).
2. John Bailey (Newcastle).
3. Glynn Snodin (Sheffield Wednesday).
4. Noel Blake (Leeds United).
5. Tony Adams (Arsenal).
6. John Wark (Ipswich).
7. Peter Reid (Everton).
8. Neil McNab (Manchester City).
9. Peter Beardsley (Liverpool).
10. Ian Rush (Juventus).
11. Alan Harper (Sheffield Wednesday).

Subs: George Reilly (West Bromwich Albion), Eric Gates (Sunderland), David Platt (Aston Villa), Nigel Vaughan (Wolves).

The Liverpool Legend

The spirit of Bill Shankly still lives at Anfield and will continue to do so for as long as Liverpool Football Club exists. Even those of us who were never fortunate enough to play under him are constantly aware of his presence, through the training routines and the many other innovations he brought to the club, as he took them from the Second to First Division, FA Cup and European Cup success. Bob Paisley, Joe Fagan and now Kenny Dalglish have carried on his work wonderfully, but it was the legendary Shanks who laid the foundations for all that has been achieved since.

I know I would have loved him because of his wicked sense of fun and his dry sense of humour but, sadly, I met him only once at our Melwood training ground, when he said to me in that familiar, gruff voice, 'Keep it going, big man.' A week later he was dead and the world had lost one of its truly great characters. Not just a great manager but a great man as well.

But let's not weep for him. Instead let us remember him for what he was and what he did, not only for Liverpool but for the beautiful game as well — and what better way than through the fund of stories that seems to have grown over the years, until the distinction between fact and fiction blurs. It doesn't matter, because it ensures that his memory will live on, and what is more it will be happy with stories told and retold wherever football people meet.

The permanent reminder for all the current Liverpool players is the sign stating 'This is Anfield' over the players' tunnel on the way from the dressing-room to the pitch. This, even more than the Shankly Gates, is his, for it was after a discussion with Bob Paisley that he decided to have it put up, because he recognised that the special atmosphere of Liverpool can lift the good professionals while putting the bad ones under pressure. Shankly and Paisley counted up and reckoned there were more bad than good — so up went the sign.

Apparently, he used to lurk around the corridor by the sign on match days, studying the opposition, noting how they were dressed, if they had all shaved, if anyone looked at all nervous, how they walked in case anyone was hiding an injury . . . and generally intimidating the opposition in his own inimitable way.

He even did it at Wembley before Liverpool played Arsenal in the 1971 Cup Final, shaking his head towards the wet Wembley pitch and saying to Bob Wilson, 'Jesus Christ son, its slippery. Verra slippery. Terrible conditions those for goalkeepers.' For once, though, it didn't work, and the Gunners beat the Reds 2–1 after extra time, with Bob handling everything well – despite the conditions.

But more often than not, this working man's psychologist and home-spun philosopher would make his point. Larger-than-life Malcolm MacDonald tried to put one over on Shanks when he saw him standing by the 'This is Anfield' sign, saying in a loud stage whisper to his manager, Joe Harvey, that they had found the right ground. Shanks immediately launched himself through the home dressing-room door to tell his players how that loud-mouth MacDonald had been deriding Liverpool Football Club and how he and the rest of the team needed a sharp lesson. Ninety minutes later Liverpool had won by three clear goals.

A young Kevin Keegan benefited when he was preparing to take on England's World Cup-winning skipper, Bobby Moore, in the heart of the West Ham defence. Having watched the Hammers stroll in, Shanks took his £30,000 striker to one side and began with the inevitable, 'Jesus Christ son, I've just seen Bobby Moore.'

Sure he now had Keegan's attention, he continued, 'Big bags under his eyes, limping, anyone can see he was out night clubbing again. You can tell. He's scared stiff of you, son. You will run him silly today.' Whereupon Keegan went out, scored a fine goal and had an outstanding game, the feature of which was his duel with the immaculate Moore. As he arrived back in the dressing-room, Shankly pulled him to one side, saying, 'What a great player that Bobby Moore is – you'll never play against a better player than him!'

Even before teams arrived the psychological war would begin. Although Liverpool have always had their opposition watched in advance, very rarely is much information passed on to the players, with the philosophy always being to let the opposition worry about us. But Shanks liked to stand in front of a table with two teams of Subbuteo players in front of him, one in red, of course, and the other in white. More often than not he would sweep the opposing forwards off the pitch and concentrate on going through the opposition defence, usually saying how poor, vulnerable or slow they were, or just, 'Forget about him . . . he can't play.'

Manchester United were always special opponents – and still are – so I can imagine the rivalry between Bill Shankly and Sir Matt Busby. I can also visualise Shanks's problems in dismissing opponents of the calibre of George Best, Bobby Charlton and Denis Law. By all accounts the figures would either finish in his

Once again Bruce Grobbelaar goes right over the top

7

pockets or be swept to the dressing-room floor. On another occasion he told the Liverpool boys how good they were and how weak United were, even predicting that United were so poor that Matt might keep them in Manchester and concede the points.

He then demolished the entire United team, starting with goalkeeper Alex Stepney being too slow to catch a cold, Tony Dunne who couldn't tackle a fish supper, through to the blind gnome Nobby Stiles and the deceptively slow Paddy Crerand, until he got

So slow he couldn't catch a cold

to the big three. He conceded Charlton, Law and Best could play but added: 'You've only got three to beat, and if you can't do that you're not professionals.' Next time the lot went on the floor.

His usual opening was: 'Christ, I've just seen the other team coming in boys. They've been out on the tiles all night and they look frightened to death.' How many of the players believed all this hype was never recorded, but the results spoke for themselves – home or abroad.

The Belgian millionaire club, Anderlecht, have always been formidable opponents, but were especially so in the mid-1960s when Liverpool were drawn against them in the second round of the European Cup. Shankly dispensed with any sort of tactical talk, though his team selection of Tommy Smith as an extra defender to allow Gordon Milne more freedom was revolutionary. 'Don't worry about this team, boys,' he said. 'They are a load of rubbish.' They might have been as well, because the Reds swept them off the park just as Shanks might have done with his models. When they filed back to the dressing-room, he met them at the door and owned up: 'Congratulations. You have just beaten one of the best teams in Europe.'

What's more, they did it again in Brussels, although it was not to be Liverpool's year that time, because they eventually went out to Italian giants Inter-Milan in most controversial and – as expected with Shanks involved – hilarious circumstances. Liverpool were miffed when a perfectly good goal was disallowed by the Austrian referee, which would have given them a 4–1 buffer to take with them to northern Italy.

On arrival in Italy, the team were faced at the airport with banners claiming they were on drugs, and everyone, particularly Shanks, was put on his guard for any underhand tricks. Bill thought he had found one that very night as the team settled into bed in their hotel on the banks of Lake Como. The hotel was next to a church whose bells pealed out their message, every hour on the hour, infuriating the boss who believed it would keep his players awake. Here accounts of the story differ, but they all agree that Shanks marched round to the church to confront the priest, who explained that nothing personal was intended and that those same bells had been ringing out for hundreds of years. Bob Paisley claims that Shanks then volunteered for him to climb the bell tower to bandage the bell and muffle the sound. Happily for Bob, if the account is true, that suggestion was also turned down.

The players claimed next day that they had heard nothing anyway. But there the fun ended, for the players were abused and spat at, and when the game got under way a succession of outrageous decisions meant that Liverpool lost in the most bitter circumstances imaginable. This probably explains why Shanks was always so suspicious of going abroad after that.

He always watched what the players ate and drank, careful that no one tried to poison them but also wanting them to have what they wanted. In Romania some of his team wanted Coca Cola with their evening meals, but were told by the waiter that there was none, only mineral water. Shanks was not impressed, particularly as he had seen someone drinking what looked suspiciously like the famous American soft drink on another table. Up he jumped and, as bold as brass, walked straight into the kitchen where he found a crate of the precious drink. Confronting the surprised waiter with the evidence, he demanded that his players got what they ordered – or he would personally inform the Kremlin.

Another time he attacked an innocent waiter, demanding to know why he had served one of his players with orange juice so near to his bed time. 'I'm not having my player spoiling his beauty sleep', said Shanks, 'by having him get up in the middle of the night for a pee!'

The surprising fact was that, while it was almost understandable that Shanks should be wary of the Europeans, everyone assumed he would love the United States with the same language (well, almost), their simple food, their boxers and the film star gangsters like Jimmy Cagney. He didn't, but that was probably because there was nobody to talk to about football and, even when he proudly wore his Liverpool blazer and badge, no one recognised him.

Yet when he couldn't talk about football, he was always happy to discuss the great boxers of his day, particularly the Americans and especially the great Jack Dempsey. In fact, when Liverpool were in Chicago he took a group of five to Soldier's Field Stadium, where he sought out the groundsman and asked him to point to the exact spot where Dempsey had fought Gene Tunney in their classic world heavyweight title fight. Who else but Shanks would then arrange a three-a-side kick-about game where the ring had been situated?

He loved Dempsey did Shanks, to the extent that when he discovered that he and another favourite, Joe Louis, lived and trained on steak, it became the staple diet for generations of Liverpool players. But not even the prospect of meeting his boxing hero could shift this stubborn man from his set ways.

During his first tour of the States in 1964, Bob Paisley met him in the lobby to take him to Dempsey's bar in New York, but Shanks shook his head, declaring it far too late. When Bob pointed out that it was only 6.30, Bill again shook his head, insisting that as far as he was concerned it was 11.30 and time for bed. No damn Yankee was going to tell him what time it was. His watch was still set to English time.

Every single Liverpool captain has been credited with the story of coming off at half-time, two goals down, to be confronted by an angry Shankly who demanded to know why he had kicked in the direction he did.

'Because I lost the toss,' answered the bowed skipper.

'What did you call?' asked Shanks.

'Heads.'

'Ah! There you are,' responded the Liverpool manager as though he had discovered the splitting of the atom. 'You should never call heads, son, always call tails.'

But perhaps the most famous and repeated story of all concerns a certain five-a-side game. Now these games were and still are the centre-piece of Liverpool's training, and in those days the games tended to go on and on, either until his team won or they were too far behind to retrieve the situation. This particular game was very tight and had gone on for so long that everyone agreed that the next goal would be the last. Now these games were always played on a pitch with goals marked out by poles, and no crossbar. Inevit-

ably, there were always disputes, but when an opponent's shot beat the goal-minder in this game, Shanks argued black was white that it went over the bar. Everyone had a different opinion until Bill turned to Chris Lawler, who was such a quiet man that he was known as 'Silent Knight'. Everyone waited with bated breath for Lawler's utterance: 'Sorry boss, it was a goal.' Shankly, amazed, gradually turned puce and exploded, 'Jesus Christ son, you've been here for ten years and not said a word. Then the first word you speak you tell a lie!'

Sometimes a goalkeeper needs to take the weight off his feet

Shanks normally liked Chrissie because he was never injured, for Shanks couldn't stand injured players of any sort. Even those with broken limbs he treated with contempt, keeping them away from his fit players in case it was catching. Chris was halfway through a run of 350 consecutive games when he collected a nasty kick on the ankle, and on the following Monday Bob Paisley, who was also the physiotherapist, told him not to train but to go off and jog on his own. As he moved off, Shanks emerged from his office to ask Bob, 'What's wrong with that malingerer?'

Shankly equally hated himself when he was injured – put out of action with a cartilage operation and, later, an ankle injury, which kept him grumpily on the sidelines for almost a month. It wouldn't have been so bad, but he wouldn't even let the others play five-a-side until he was fit and ready to play in them himself.

Yet the players always came first with him, and he once said, 'I am a people's man, a players' man. You could call me a humanist.' No one who knew him would disagree.

He would not stand a word against his boys from anyone – not even directors of the club. One so enraged him with his comments concerning a particular player during a game that he stormed into the board room to make his feelings known, until someone nudged him to point out that the butt of the complaints was standing directly behind him. Spinning on his heel, Shanks fixed him with a gimlet eye and said, 'Aye, that's the bugger I'm talking about.'

Mind you, he was a bit different to the players' faces, and many a top international felt the rough edge of his sandpaper tongue. Secretly he got on best with those who had a go back at him when he was in the wrong. Which was probably why he had such an outstanding relationship with Tommy Smith, and

also why the players used to send Tommy into the boot room to argue any points on their behalf. One row of mammoth proportions came to a halt in hysterical laughter when Shankly suddenly shouted at Smithy, 'You! You'd start a riot in a cemetery!'

He was so sensitive to the outside world about his players that when questioned by the Press about axing certain individuals, he would respond, 'I don't drop players. I make changes.'

He worried about their home life and even their sex life. Anyone who wanted to marry in the middle of the season was looked upon with total contempt, scotching stories that he took his wife, Nessie, to see Accrington Stanley on the anniversary of their marriage.

'That was ridiculous,' he sniffed. 'It was her birthday, and it wasn't Accrington Stanley, it was their reserves.'

As for sex before football, Shanks was philosophical: 'Of course a player can have relations with his wife before a match and still play a blinder. But if he did it every time for six months he'd be a decrepit old man. It saps the strength from the body.'

He was certainly concerned about Phil Thompson's somewhat skeletal frame as a youngster. Shanks immediately used the boxers' philosophy of steak for breakfast, steak for lunch and steak for supper.

'We have got to build this lad up if he is going to be a centre half,' growled Shanks. 'I've seen more meat on a butcher's pencil.' Some time later a request reached Shanks that Phil wanted to break the cardinal rule and get married during the season and, to compound his crime, he wanted a day off to do the vile deed.

'Jesus Christ,' exploded Shanks. 'We've bred a monster.'

The players he liked least were those who were foolish enough to turn him and his beloved Liverpool down. He could never quite believe it, especially when he had gone as far as putting a fatherly arm around their shoulders and showing them round Anfield. Huddersfield full back Bob McNab was told he would be joining the greatest club in the world with the best players, the best facilities and the best fans. Shanks told McNab he was a quality player and expected him to respond by signing on the dotted line there and then. He was therefore surprised when McNab asked for a little time to think, and even more surprised later to receive a telephone call from McNab with the news that he had signed for Arsenal. Before slamming the phone down, Shankly snapped, 'Och, They are welcome to you. You never could play the game anyway.'

Even worse was the day that little Lou Macari decided to join his rival, Matt Busby, at Manchester United. Macari was due to move to Anfield from Celtic in a blaze of publicity but he, like McNab, begged time and said that as United had made an official approach it would only be courteous to talk to them. Shanks was still confident of his latest capture when he breezed into the dressing-room and saw the banner headlines on the tabloid press, left deliberately for the benefit of his gaze, informing the world that Macari had gone to Old Trafford. Shanks brushed the papers to one side with the bald statement: 'He was never that good. I was only buying him for our reserve team.'

Shanks also had other dislikes. Notably referees. If Shankly had been quoted verbatim by the Press, he would have faced Football Association disciplinary committees every other week, for he used to equate the men in black with a certain little German with a toothbrush moustache and a funny haircut. During one of the many referee clamp-downs, Shanks let his true feelings be known when he said in a quieter moment, 'The trouble with referees is that they know the rules but they don't know the game.'

Neither did he like opponents who threatened Liverpool's growing majesty. On the eve of the Derby County and Manchester City game in 1972, when both teams were contesting the League Championship with Liverpool, Shankly met and shook hands with City manager Joe Mercer, saying, 'I hope you both lose.' Anything was possible to Shanks.

Of course, Everton were his pet hate and he would always say, 'There are two great teams on Merseyside – Liverpool and Liverpool reserves,' and 'If Everton were playing at the bottom of my garden I wouldn't bother to draw the curtains.'

His favourite bit of mischief was the apocryphal tale of the 1966 FA Cup Final and a supposed conversation between Princess Margaret and the Everton captain, Brian Labone. According to Shanks, the conversation went like this:

Princess Margaret: 'But, Mr Labone, where is Everton?'

Brian Labone: 'In Liverpool, Ma'am.'

Princess Margaret: 'Of course. We had your first team here last year.'

One thing on which everyone agreed was that Bill Shankly was a big, warm-hearted man who loved almost every-one. He certainly had his heroes – notably Denis Law, Sir Matt Busby and the late Jock Stein. He was one of the first in the dressing-room after Celtic's great European Cup triumph against Inter-Milan in 1967, bursting in, grasp-ing the Big Man by the hand and saying for all to hear: 'John, You're immortal.' One legend to another!

The one he loved and respected best of all was not even a Scot but an Englishman, a Preston North End team-mate – the genuinely great Tom Finney. He would talk about him at the drop of the hat, and few could compare in his mind. When a bold journalist once tried to get Shanks to agree that a current wing hero was in the same class, Shanks thought about it for a few moments and conceded, 'Aye, you may be right, but remember Tom is 60 now!' Wind Shanks up about Tom and away he would go: 'Tom Finney was grizzly strong. He could run for a week!'

'I would have played him in my team in an overcoat.'

'There would be four of the opposi-tion marking him when we were kick-ing in.'

'When I told people in Scotland that England were coming up with a winger who was better than Stanley Matthews,

they laughed at me. But they weren't bloody laughing when big George Young was running all over Hampden Park looking for a man named Tom Finney.'

Shanks must have been some char-acter as a player as well. Everyone says he was a non-stop, physical wing half, feared rather than loved by his rivals. Perhaps that was where he learned how to intimidate opposing teams as a manager, for he told the tale himself of how a young player known as Boy Baston of Arsenal came to Deepdale with a growing reputation, and Shanks wanted no nonsense that might tarnish his proud international record. At the first opportunity he sidled up to the Gunners player with the warning, 'None of your tricks, son, or you will finish up on your arse on the track.' Baston's response was to sell Shanks a big dummy, fly past him and set Arsenal on the attack. Shanks caught up with him at a throw-in and growled in his best Cagney voice: 'Any more of that, son, and you will be in real trouble.'

So Shanks couldn't believe it when Baston again jinked his way past him and continued to do so for the remain-der of the first half, despite his marker coming out with every conceivable word of intimidation. As the half-time whistle blew a tired, breathless Shank-ly mentioned to a nearby Arsenal player how brave the boy Baston was and how he had ignored every threat Shanks had made. The Arsenal player fell about, catching his breath just long enough to tell the stunned Scot, 'Don't you know, Bill – he's stone deaf!'

When he eventually quit and handed over his famous number four shirt to

Tommy Docherty, he remarked: 'Just put it on and it will run around by itself.' Certainly some of that raw Scots humour rubbed off on the recipient of that famous shirt.

Bill Shankly developed a great understanding of the men around him, treating his original group of players like family, even to the point of showing them blatant favouritism, as he did when Ron Yeats and Ian St John missed a curfew after a friendly in Dublin. Shanks called in Ron Yeats first and listened to his string of excuses before letting him off with a mild rebuke. As he left, Yeats asked if he should send in the Saint.

'No need, son,' responded Shanks. 'He'll only tell me the same pack of lies.'

He wasn't really surprised at his fellow Scots having a few wee drams after a game, but he was staggered when, of all people, the saintly Ian Callaghan arrived back at the team hotel in Belgium with the usual group of lively party-goers. They all took the customary dressing down before Shankly rounded on Callaghan with, 'And as for you Callaghan, you of all people . . . I'm . . . I'm . . . I'm going to tell your wife on you!'

His forceful character usually meant he would get his own way, whoever was involved, as two little old ladies discovered in a hotel in Porthcawl before a game at Swansea. All the way from Merseyside Shanks had been going on about an Ali fight to be shown on television that night, advising everyone to make straight

for the television lounge as soon as the team arrived. But there they were confronted by two old dears, perched in front of the television ready for their injection of *Coronation Street*, and suddenly surrounded by Shanks and fourteen or so large young men. On the basis of first come first served, they looked to have won a rare victory over Bill Shankly until inspiration hit him and he called for a democratic vote, which he knew he would win 15−2. Exit two rather peeved old ladies.

They shouldn't have minded; he was like that with everyone. God help anyone who crossed his path, whoever it was. He even took issue with the groundsman at Orient when a game was called off because the pitch was waterlogged. It didn't suit his plans to have to make an extra and, as he thought, unnecessary trip to London. Calling over the poor groundsman, he told him, 'The trouble with your ground is that you have ordinary grass. Come up to Anfield and see our pitch. We've got professional grass.'

He was also impulsive on occasions, such as on a trip he and Bob Paisley made to Lincoln to watch a goalkeeper. They stopped for a bite to eat during their four-hour journey and, as a consequence, arrived late for the game. The goalkeeper they were watching

had scarcely a back pass to pick up, never mind a save, but after a quarter of an hour Shanks announced that he had seen enough and they left. He never did tell Bob what he saw to turn him off in those fifteen minutes, and all I can say is thank goodness he wasn't with Bob when he watched me at Crewe. I might still be in Canada if first impressions counted that much.

On another occasion, the religious freak took up his usual position outside Anfield, brandishing his placard, proclaiming 'Repent or be doomed for ever'. This time he plucked up the courage to approach the great man, enquiring: 'Mr Shankly have you repented yet? What will you do if the Lord comes?' Shanks scarcely broke stride as he shot back: 'Move Ian St John to the left wing.'

Inside the ground he could be just as cutting. An expensive new striker had gone missing during a particularly rugged local derby against Everton. Everyone waited for the blast, but instead Shanks beckoned the player and, putting his arm round him, took him down the tunnel and on to the pitch. Not a word did he say to the puzzled centre forward as they traversed Anfield from side to side, corner to corner, until the player could restrain himself no longer and asked, 'What are we looking for, boss?' Shanks finally looked up and replied: 'We're looking for the hole you hid in this afternoon.'

He could be scathing about opponents and his own players alike. 'Play like you've never played before,' he told one young reserve whom he had to play because of injuries. 'Play well.'

If that made the poor lad cringe, what about his remark after another game: 'My right half was magic today – he kept disappearing all afternoon.'

Or: 'My outside right was so slow the linesman went past him.'

One man who would hold his own with Shanks was Bob Paisley. There was the classic day when Tony Hateley, father of England striker Mark, was having rather a bad day. Nothing was going right for him, with the ball bouncing off his shin, ankle and knees, as he continually lost possession and failed even to get in his usual fine headers. Finally, he went down injured, and before he could rise to his feet, Bob was on the pitch waving for the St John Ambulance men to follow him with the stretcher. Tony's legs were strapped together and, told by Bob to lie still, he was disappearing down the tunnel as Shanks rushed down from the stand asking: 'What's the matter?'

Bob turned to him. 'He's okay. I'm just making sure that when I get him off you don't send him back.'

My favourite Shankly story – and we all have one – was one that rebounded on the great man. The team were on their way to a European match in Iceland, flying from Prestwick, God's own country as far as Bill Shankly was concerned. With the bus taking the team to Ayrshire, he was determined that all should see and fully appreciate the beauty of the Scottish countryside. The only problem was that they got lost, and eventually the exasperated Shankly, claiming he could speak the local language, stopped the coach to hail a passing cyclist.

'We're Liverpool Football Club and we are on our way to Reykjavik,' said Shanks, somewhat pompously.

'Well you are on the wrong road for sure,' said the man, cycling off and leaving Shankly's face as red as his tie.

He was, above all, a man of the people, aware of the fans – particularly those faithful who stood on the Kop week in and week out. He reached out for them, feeling that with Liverpool he was doing something for them and the community. He loved them and they loved him; they were on the same wavelength. After Liverpool had beaten Newcastle to win the FA Cup at Wembley, two Scousers rushed out on to the sacred turf, prostrated themselves and kissed his feet. Looking down with an amused smile, Shanks said, 'While you're down there, lads, give my shoes a quick polish.'

Once in Belfast to watch a match at Windsor Park, he was asked whether he had flown or caught the ferry.

'I flew,' said Shanks. 'But don't make it public, because in Liverpool they think I walk here.'

They did and still do. Bill Shankly's name lives on and long may it do so to give everyone a smile and a memory. To end with his most famous quote: 'Some people think football is a matter of life and death. I don't like that attitude. I can assure them it is much more serious than that.'

This is Anfield

There is no greater club in the world than Liverpool FC. Although it is often called 'the big red machine', there is nothing mechanical about the players and the people who make up the components. Everyone is an individual and a character in his own right and here's the proof.

Tartan Mafia

Steve Nicol is about the nicest guy in the entire dressing-room, not to mention one of the best players. But he is also the most put upon because he is a touch – shall we say – gullible. The Scottish mafia were always hard on him, and whenever they travelled together to play for their country he would inevitably be the butt of their jokes.

There was the famous occasion when he, Souness, Dalglish and Hansen were driving north to an international in the middle of a snow storm. Stopping, they asked him to get something from the boot – and the ever-obliging Steve, dressed only in track suit bottoms and T-shirt jumped out – only to be left shivering on the side of the road for ten minutes when they drove off.

Chico, as he is affectionately known, is a goffer for the Tartan Army, but no one else. When he roomed with me I couldn't sleep for the crackling of crisp packets and the hiss of the ring pulls of Coca Cola cans. Then in the morning I couldn't get to the sink to shave because of the empty cans. He wouldn't take any notice of me, but would always be ready to defend his fellow Scots, claiming that they were the foundation of the club's success – until I pointed out that the first European Cup triumph against the Germans of Borussia Moenchengladbach was achieved without a single Scot in the entire team. He had to look it up before he would believe me.

The team then was: Ray Clemence (England), Phil Neal (England), Joey Jones (Wales), Tommy Smith (England), Ray Kennedy (England), Emlyn Hughes (England), Kevin Keegan (England), Jimmy Case (England), Steve Heighway (Republic of Ireland), Ian Callaghan (England), Terry McDermott

(England), Manager – Bob Paisley (England) . . . not a Jock in sight, with Hansen, Souness and Dalglish not appearing until the successful defence of the trophy against FC Bruges at Wembley the next year.

Souness, the original mafia Godfather because of his strong personality, was succeeded by that intellectual, Jocky Hansen, mastermind of the team, the man whose word ended all arguments . . . whether he was right or wrong! Nothing throws him; he's cooler than the freezer compartment in the fridge, retaining his calm exterior and cutting sarcasm in the heat of the fiercest battle. When I dropped the ball for the goal that led to our European exit against the Poles of Widzew Lodz he remarked, 'Nice catch, Brucie – better luck next year.'

When Phil Thompson made a mistake in a European Cup Final he didn't rollock him, but merely spent the next 20 minutes taking the mickey.

He could get away with it because he earned the respect of us all with his outstanding ability, being not only one of our best players but also one of the best in Europe. No one at Liverpool could believe it when he was left out of Scotland's squad for the Mexico World Cup. I should think temporary manager Alex Ferguson still has nightmares about that one.

He is a good leader on the field, but not always the best captain off it, because if he thinks something doesn't concern him he won't do anything about it. I found it much easier to take a problem to Souness.

It is also unlikely that the Round Table of Swaziland will ever invite Jocky back after his exhibition of football skills rather than diplomacy when he was auctioning signed footballs on an end-of-season tour. The generous bidder stood up to collect his expensive prize from the captain of Liverpool, only to have the football volleyed at him from the top table. The best that could be said of that incident was that Jocky was as accurate as ever with his passing.

Clangers

The worst thing you can do in a Liverpool dressing-room is to get your words wrong – which let Craig Johnston and me in for a lot of punishment.

I was always dropping clangers. In Africa I brought the house down by asking for a Bacardi and Coke on the rocks with no ice. I also made a twit of myself at my belated stag party. We were in a Liverpool bar called the Panama where a black 'Jaws' was giving an exhibition of his amazing fitness with exaggerated exercises, Kung Fu kicks, squats and, finally, press-ups which began with a fall forward, arms at his sides until the last possible moment. With a few drinks inside me, I felt I could do that, keeping my arms still for even longer. I won the bet. I didn't move my arms at all, breaking my fall with my chin, so that the party was interrupted while I left for a few stitches to stop the flow of blood.

For a long time I had a quiet chuckle at the others over opening bottles of Coke with my eyebrow. It is the biggest con in the world and I have laughed myself silly reading other players' accounts of how I have left myself red-eyed doing my party trick. As I lifted the bottle, I would lever the top with my thumb and then make a hissing noise between my teeth as I supposedly prised off the top.

Craig Johnston, a man of whim and inexhaustible energy on and off the pitch, was also a frequent target of the mickey-takers. He has thrown himself into photography, into making and producing a record which cost him a fortune, rebuilding his house and, of course, into his football. He even followed the strict diets of Martina Navratilova and Ivan Lendl from their book *Eat to Win*. As a player he is underrated at Liverpool, perhaps because he is often so self-critical.

I probably know more about him than most, having shared rooms with him longer than anyone else. I have seen off David Johnson, John McGregor, Michael 'Cat' Robinson, Steve Nicol and even Graeme Souness, but Craig has survived. His mind is so active that he struggles to get off to sleep, watching television until the early hours and then taking two sleeping pills so that when he does go off, he is like a dead man. You can't hear him breathe.

Digger Barnes

Another player I rate highly as a man as well as a player is John Barnes. He's as laid back as Jocky Hansen, and when the other players started on the usual bit about Jungle Man seeing him off, he grinned. See off Digger Barnes? They must be joking. He is a smashing bloke who is as much fun as my old room-rate in Vancouver, Carl Valentine. The fans nicknamed him 'Tarmac' – the black Heighway, which was clever but not clever enough, for he is 100 times better than the Irishman ever was, and that is not meant as an insult.

Mind you, when I first met him at Watford I thought him arrogant, although when he joined us I realised that it was simply his confidence showing through. He is as popular as Steve Nicol in the dressing-room, though he takes terrible stick over his training gear of gloves, balaclava and anything else he needs to keep warm. He really feels the cold and even has a hot bath before playing to loosen up. No wonder he wanted to play in Italy in the warm. He would have done well there too, and in fact is probably one of the few players we could successfully export to Brazil without him looking out of place in any way.

Red and Blue

There's a lot of talk about the intensity of Merseyside derby games between Everton and Liverpool, but while it is true that we love to beat each other, the real rivalry is between the supporters. Quite often you have families who are half red and half blue, which is perhaps why the rivalry rarely turns nasty. For proof you only have to recall that wonderful Milk Cup Final when the two colours were all mixed in together, singing and enjoying the occasion. It was apt that it finished as a goalless draw, with the humour retained long after the game was over. It was all quite emotional.

Even before the kick-off the fans were able to see the two teams enjoying a joke together. Ian Rush and Kevin Ratcliffe are particularly good friends, both sharing a laugh before the kick-off, on this occasion when Everton goalkeeper Neville Southall came out to look at the pitch and drink in the atmosphere, resplendent in his Cup Final suit . . . and flip-flops with no socks.

Funnier still was the clash between the two mates once the game got under way. Ian had scored a lot of goals against Everton in his time at Anfield, and Ratcliffe was determined that it was not going to happen this time in front of a world-wide television audience. He whacked Rushy twice — very hard, as if to remind him not to take liberties. Minutes later Ratcliffe was on the touchline, nose pouring blood. It looked as though murders would be committed when the Everton central defender recovered and raced straight for Rushy, only for the two of them to burst out laughing at the instant when a physical confrontation seemed inevitable.

Cheers

Terry McDermott is one of the funniest men I have ever met in my life. He didn't give a fig about anyone or anything, and would take the mickey out of everyone, including manager Bob Paisley whom he mimicked unmercifully. Legend had it that Terry Mac lived on lager and that when the time came for him to leave Anfield, he turned down a massive offer to play in France because he didn't fancy the local brew!

Once when Liverpool were taking the salute from a huge crowd gathered in front of the Town Hall, he suddenly realised that the celebratory lager he had quaffed was now seeking an exit, but he could find no way through the crowds. So what did he do? He found a quiet corner of the balcony and quietly relieved himself over the side.

He in turn was sent up on his return to Anfield with Newcastle United. Terry suffered from frequent cold sores, so on the day of the game one of our players bought a box of fake sores from a joke shop. Terry didn't twig at first, but once player after player had gone up to talk to him, each one sporting a festering sore, he suddenly realised he had been had, and dissolved into fits of helpless laughter.

Everyone talks about our runaway

success in the League under Kenny Dalglish, but they seem to forget that we did it once before, wrapping up our Championship with seven games remaining. It was Bob Paisley's last season and he wanted to go out with a bang, but the incentive had gone and we were as flat as yesterday's champagne or, more accurately, that lunchtime's Sancerre. In the end Bob had had enough and called us together for a dressing down. At least that was what was supposed to happen, but it all fell apart when Bob stormed into the room where we had gathered, pulled the curtains together with a sharp tug, and brought them crashing down on his head to cries of 'Pull yourself together Douggie'.

Nice One!

To those of us who knew them well, it was no surprise that Kenny Dalglish and Graeme Souness, room-mates with both Liverpool and Scotland, turned into successful managers, for both are winners with a mean streak inside them. There was no doubt that they got on well together but, according to Souness, it was not always the case. They first roomed together (not quite pre-war) with Scotland in West Germany. Souness had heard what a good-living, non-smoking, non-drinking, home-loving man the Celtic striker was, but it was always Souness who, despite his reputation as a fun-loving single man, was in bed and asleep before Kenny crept into bed.

It was not until the two were paired up again at Liverpool that the awful truth came out. Kenny had been told that Graeme was not just a bachelor but a bachelor gay in the most modern sense of the phrase. Having been wound up by the others, Kenny must have taken one look at the Anglo-Scot's array of toiletries and his hairdrier to convince himself that the others were telling the truth.

I used to reckon they were put together because Graeme was one of the few who could cut through Kenny's thick Glaswegian accent in those early days. Some still struggle to understand him now.

Kenny is never short of a sharp reply to any question but even 'The Boss' was struck dumb on one of our visits to Tel Aviv. He was waiting for the hotel lift when a foreign-looking lady joined him. The lift was taking an age to arrive and Kenny mumbled something to that effect in his Scottish accent. The lady looked up thinking he was talking to her and said, 'I'm sorry I only speak English.'

When asked what Kenny Dalglish's best position was in midfield or attack, the late Jock Stein responded: 'Och! Just let him on the park.'

Kenny was always modest to a fault about his own performances and particularly some of his brilliantly taken goals. But Bob Paisley recalls: 'He always called his goals taps-in until we came to the end of the season and we were talking money and new contracts. Then suddenly he changed his mind.'

There were those who doubted just how successful Kenny Dalglish would be as a manager, myself among them. But former Liverpool iron-man Tommy Smith had no hesitation in observing, 'He'll probably make a better manager than many of those about. He loves football. I see those blokes like Malcolm Allison and Terry Neill trying to fool everyone by putting on a track suit, when everyone knows that all they really want is a platform for self-promotion. Kenny's different.'

Graeme Souness had no doubts about his ability to control the players either, remarking drily, 'He would make a perfect trade union official.'

Golden Corner

Jack Charlton has never been known for producing devil-may-care fast-flowing attacking football and his Middlesbrough side of the 1970s was no exception. During one particularly mind-numbing game against Liverpool, Kevin Keegan turned to his former Anfield team-mate Phil Boersma, and stifling a yawn asked, 'What do you have up here? Golden Corner competitions?'

Bob Paisley had a marvellous gift for humour, as well as a great insight into football. He experienced more success, first with Bill Shankly and then through his own talents, than any other manager in history. But he was forced to admit: 'Mind, I've been here during the bad times as well. One year we came second.'

He also had a biting wit when opponents tried to get one up on his Liverpool team, saying, 'A lot of teams beat us, do a lap of honour – and never stop running. After Burnley had beaten us, I remember Jimmy Adamson crowing that his players were in a different League. At the end of the season they

were. They were relegated.'

Liverpool have never had any time for the yuppies of the game. FA coaching courses are not part of their style any more than modern terminology is acceptable in the boot room . . . especially with that down-to-earth Geordie, Bob Paisley. He observed: 'Some of the jargon is frightening. They talk of "getting round the back", sounding more like burglars than footballers. Then they say, "You've got to make more positive runs", or, "You're too negative". What are they? Electricians? But the people who talk like this have no real depth or knowledge of what they're really talking about.'

Big John McGrath, manager of Port Vale, was trying to raise much-needed funds by selling the tricky winger, Mark Chamberlain. His efforts eventually led to him telephoning Bob Paisley with the offer, 'I've got a player here and 300,000 won't buy him.'

'I know,' said Bob drily. 'I am one of them.'

Just like Cinderella –
always late for the ball

A Half Please

They reckoned that Tommy Smith was one of the nicest men at Liverpool, who according to his former team-mate, Ron Yeats, would always return after chopping an opponent in half to help him look for the other half.

Liverpool on Tour

Some of Liverpool's funniest moments have occurred abroad, and not just on the usual pre-season and end of season tours, either. One of the best weeks we have ever spent was immediately before our European Cup Final against Roma which, incredibly, UEFA had scheduled to be played in our opponents' stadium. Now how's that for a real sick joke? A bit like playing a two-legged game on just the one ground. Roma were whisked away to a monastic training camp on top of one of the seven hills, away from families, away from everything, coming down only at match time for their daily training session on the pitch where the final was to be played.

We, however, went to Tel Aviv for a

Clowning around

104

drink and a kick-about. Some of the Italian journalists even came with us to study our training methods, and were astonished to see us lying by the hotel pool sipping gin and tonics, and going out for a few beers in the evening.

But why not? No Championship-winning team anywhere in Europe has a tougher time than the English champions, and having won both the League Cup and the League, we were entitled to rest. Even the 'kick-about' was a game against the Israeli national XI!

That trip cost me a few quid. After we'd watched on television in the Glasgow Bar as Everton beat Watford in the FA Cup Final, ensuring that every possible piece of silverware finished back on Merseyside, I stayed on for a game of cribbage when the other lads left. By the time I had supped a few beers, I didn't really fancy the walk back to the team hotel, so I persuaded one of the guys in the bar to lend me his pushbike. Having paid little attention to the arrangements for returning the machine, I simply found a local lad, gave him a nice tip, and asked him to take the bike back to the bar. Needless to say it never arrived and cost me around £150.

What those Italian journalists must have thought of our antics I don't know, but they discovered the sort of shape we were in when we licked the local national team 4–1 – a bigger margin than England achieved against them a couple of years later.

That European Cup tie, of course, was the game that was to earn me world-wide notoriety, not for a daft mistake (although I was not happy with myself over Pruzzo's equalising header) but because of my antics in the penalty shoot-out that decided the destination of the biggest European prize of them all. Liverpool have never had a great reputation as penalty kickers, and when Steve Nicol missed the opening spot kick we were up to our chins in it with the crocodiles snapping. Manager Joe Fagan had given me the idea when he told me not to worry, that there was nothing a goalkeeper could do in these circumstances, just to try and put them off. So when the Italian international, Conti, came up to take his shot, I put my hands on my knees and did my own version of the 'Black Bottom' dance routine. The Italians were livid and complained bitterly to the officials, but I had stayed within the rules by keeping my feet firmly on the ground until he shot.

It had worked once so why not a second time? This time it was top striker Graziani, and as he prepared for his crucial penalty, I kept him waiting while I gnawed at the netting in the back of my goal. Then, wandering back to my line, I looked him straight in the eye and he crossed himself. He must have seen a bit of the jungle when he looked at me, and I knew I had wrested the advantage from him. I let myself go loose, wobbling my knees, letting my arms hang down and my head loll about on my chest like some grotesque rag doll about to collapse in a heap on the floor. From the moment he ran up to take it, I knew he had it all wrong.

I didn't even have to dive. I had done my bit without having to make one save, and the 'clown' suddenly enjoyed an international audience.

That was one of the secrets of our success that season – everything was such a laugh. That European Cup Final, played in Rome as it was, should have been one of the all-time pressure games, but our stint in Tel Aviv had worked wonders, and we remained un-ruffled, even when we were hassled on our way into Rome.

Chin-Chin

We had taken the precaution of using our own 'minder', the inscrutable Tony Chinn – a martial arts expert who stayed awake all night at the end of the corridor in the hotel to ensure that our beauty sleep was undisturbed by evil-minded Italians or amorous wives or girlfriends.

It looked as though the plan and Tony had failed when our two key players, skipper Graeme Souness and Kenny Dalglish, were woken by a tele-vision blaring from the room next door. They were furious, banging on the wall, telephoning the room and even hammering on the door, waking up a few more of us in the process. Nothing worked, and in the end they called trainer Roy Evans, who was equally unsuc-cessful. He and Tony Chinn were about to batter down the door when the noise abruptly ceased and everyone retired.

Souness and Dalglish, leaving their room for breakfast next morning, were still discussing their deaf neighbour when the door next to them opened and out walked the offender – manager Joe Fagan. As the two players stared at him open mouthed, Souness was first to recover, asking, 'Didn't you hear the telephone last night?'

'Yes,' replied Joe. 'But I thought it would only be more of those cheeky Italian journalists. So I ignored it.'

'Didn't you hear us banging on the door?' asked Dalglish.

'Of course,' said Joe. 'But I wasn't expecting anyone at that time of night and I was ready for bed.'

'Well,' persisted the frustrated Sou-ness, 'didn't you hear Kenny and me banging on the wall?'

'No,' came the thoughtful response. 'Probably because I had the television on rather loud!'

It all helped to keep us giggling, and by the time the final came round we were so relaxed that when Graeme Souness prepared to wind us up like a good captain should we were ready for anything. 'Come on lads,' he said. 'Let's buzz.' Everyone started to make buzzing noises. It sounded like a bee farm, and as we ran out for the start we were all grinning like idiots.

Madison Square Garden

Tel Aviv was always a good place for Liverpool to relax, although now and again we were guilty, perhaps, of relax-ing too much. One of the root causes of our problems on one occasion was a game called 'buzz', something most social drinkers will recognise. During a bout, Ian Rush suddenly fell to the floor, and although he managed it un-aided, his mate Dave Hodgson flew into a rage, demanding to know who had pushed his friend. He didn't wait to find out but laid into the pack, throwing punches. Alan Kennedy caught a punch in the face and I found Hodgy on my back. Instincts die hard and, as my army training took over, I only just managed to stop myself in time to save Hodgy from some severe punishment.

The 'rumble' stopped almost as soon as it had begun and Hodgy, along with Rush, Ronnie Whelan and John McGregor began to wend their way back to the hotel, only to tumble down some steep steps, landing in a tangle of arms and legs at the feet of director Mr S. T. Moss, JP, who was on his way to discover what the noise was about. In response to his angry enquiry as to what was happening, Geordie Hodgy extricated himself, grinned up at Mr Moss and said: 'Whay aye Mossy yer old bugger you, you and me are just the same you know.'

It all ended in tears — tears of laughter — and when Bob Paisley called the offenders in front of him, wanting to know who had been fighting, the chorus of 'Not us boss' was accepted, despite the cuts, bruises and black eyes. After the game that night, everyone went back to the same bar, but the petrified manager needn't have worried; lessons, for a while anyway, had been learned. The square where it happened, though, has since become known as Madison Square Garden!

Sarcasm is the staple diet of most footballers' wit, followed closely by leg-pulling — often of the wickedest nature. The very worst, but conversely one of the most successful, was pulled on Steve Nicol on one of those Israeli trips. Steve, as usual, was a natural target for a wind-up expert of the quality of Alan 'Jocky' Hansen.

Steve's great hero, Kenny Dalglish, had been a bit out of sorts and playing below his usual high standards. Steve was so concerned about it that Jocky took him to one side and explained that Kenny had recently been told he was suffering from a terminal disease and did not have long to live. Everyone except Steve knew about the send-up, so that wherever he turned for confirmation he was met with sombre faces and sad words. He was so distraught that eventually he could resist it no longer and approached Kenny himself for the ultimate confirmation, which the cruel Kenny not only gave but embellished by asking Steve if he hadn't noticed the changes in him, the weight loss, the poor form. . . .

It was only then that the whole joke was exposed, with everyone cracking up as Steve, near to tears by this time, nodded sagely and said, 'Yes, now you come to mention it, I have wondered why you have been playing so badly.'

Biggest Dummy

The best send-up I ever saw was in Bucharest in Romania when Graeme Souness sold a dummy to an entire crowd of 70,000 hostile football supporters who were howling for his blood. They were waiting for him after the first leg of our game against the hard nuts of Dynamo Bucharest, who had kicked lumps out of us in front of our own fans at Anfield until their biggest thug, Movila, left the pitch clutching a broken jaw, claiming that our captain had punched him.

The intimidation began as soon as we arrived at Bucharest Airport, where even the police were making threatening gestures, and when we ran out in the pouring rain we were pelted with debris. Souness was, of course, the focal point of the attention and the booing and jeering grew louder every time he touched the ball in the warm-up. Never the sort to miss the chance of a good leg-pull, the other players realised that the skipper was the target and so everyone who received the ball from him would immediately give it back until a huge circle had formed with 'Charlie' in the middle. The crowd were now almost at fever pitch and the noise grew to a frightening crescendo as yet another ball rolled towards him — only for Souness to produce the classic dummy, causing them to break off in mid boo and leaving the rest of us curled up with laughter.

Again, it helped to relax us, and Souness had the last laugh by giving Ian Rush the pass for the goal which took us towards the European Cup Final in Rome. But that was one occasion when everyone was grateful to be catching the plane home straight after the game.

Not that we could have cared less as we left that rain-sodden pitch and joyfully made our way to the dressing-room. The laughter suddenly stopped when our manager at the time, Joe Fagan, walked in, looking like a politi-

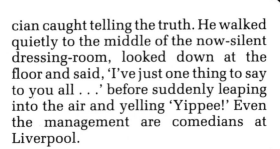

cian caught telling the truth. He walked quietly to the middle of the now-silent dressing-room, looked down at the floor and said, 'I've just one thing to say to you all . . .' before suddenly leaping into the air and yelling 'Yippee!' Even the management are comedians at Liverpool.

European Cup ties were also a great source of fun on the rare occasions when we could stay on after games. More often than not we were whipped home straight after games on Wednesday night, but happily there were the exceptions, like Greece and Portugal,

where games kicked off so late in the afternoon that it was impracticable to return home on the same day, giving us the opportunity for a night out on foreign soil.

Lisbon is always an ideal place for celebrating a good European victory because most teams stay out on the coastal resort of Estoril, with its abundance of good restaurants and easy-to-drink Vinho Verde. We played Benfica of Lisbon twice in quick succession and the first time listened with envy to accounts of the spectacular fish meal Graeme Souness and Michael Robinson had enjoyed in a Cascais establishment, kept open specially for their benefit.

They call him Teflon – the non-stick goalkeeper

The next time most of the team went there and enjoyed lobster, crab, oysters and every other form of Crustacea you could imagine, washed down with quantities of the 'green wine'. Everyone, that is, except the circumspect Mark Lawrenson, who contented himself with a bowl of tomato soup, a Dover sole and chips. No one took any notice until the bill arrived and was, as usual, divided equally. Lawrenson took one look at his £60 share and grumbled, 'That is the most expensive fish and chips I've ever had. It's the last time I come out with you lot!'

A Greek taverna gave Ian Rush the opportunity to display his Zorba dancing skills in Athens after we had beaten Panathinaikos, and he was so carried away with the Retsina and the dancing that he did not notice when a local broke half-a-dozen plates over his head, rather than throwing them on the floor. Rushy did nothing, just clapped, but so close were our little group that the offending Greek left with a severe headache.

Wrong Room

Liverpool players were not always conspicuous as super-star members of one of the world's great sporting teams. On a pre-season tour to Spain once, Jocky Hansen, unable to play because of injury, tried to walk across the pitch in Marbella to join us at half time, but was restrained by a diligent policeman who, when our skipper tried to explain who he was, hit him in the mouth.

Mind you, Jocky could hardly complain because he was equally guilty of mistaken identity in Israel. After a particularly heavy lunchtime session, he excused himself and headed back to our hotel for a siesta. Weaving into reception, he picked up the key to 509, only to return ten minutes later, complaining bitterly that they had given him the key to someone else's room. He calmed down only when it was gently pointed out to him that he was in the Diplomat and wanted the Ramada next door. Still, those hotels along the front in Tel Aviv do look rather similar.

Big Star

There are no stars at Liverpool, as Craig Johnston discovered to his cost. When we drew 0–0 with Bilbao in the European Cup and looked to be heading for certain defeat in northern Spain, their coach described Craig as the biggest star in our galaxy, praising his skills and form to the local Press. The only problem was that someone forgot to tell our manager, Joe Fagan, about it and he left Craig on the bench as Liverpool swept gloriously through to the next round.

The First Trophies

My travel has always been blighted by the fact that I was born in Africa and needed work permits until I was granted a British passport. When I started to try to start my English career with West Bromwich Albion and Bournemouth, I had insurmountable problems over obtaining a work permit. Needless to say Liverpool had no such difficulties once they had agreed to pay a quarter of a million pounds to Vancouver Whitecaps for me. The only minor hitch was that I had already entered the country to conclude the personal terms of the contract and officially to sign on the dotted line. I should have passed through immigration with all the documents up to date and properly stamped, so technically I suppose I was an illegal immigrant.

Liverpool had it all worked out that I should fly to Paris, stay for 24 hours and re-enter the country properly with everything that was needed. Bob Paisley told me to return to Anfield to pick up my air tickets, but if it looked as though there were any reporters or photographers around I was to stay in the taxi, turn back, and wait at the hotel for further instructions. For obvious reasons they didn't want anyone to know that Jungle Man as already in town.

Needless to say, when the taxi pulled into Anfield, the place was swarming with reporters and, flattered, I ordered the driver to take me back. He must have thought I was barmy. More than likely I could have stepped out, picked up my tickets and left without being noticed, for the media had gathered for the signing of another South African-born player, Craig Johnston, whose journey to Anfield was almost as complex as mine, involving Australia and Middlesbrough.

The tickets duly arrived at the hotel and I flew from Manchester's Ringway Airport to Charles de Gaulle, where I was asked for my visa for entry into France. Now that was something even Liverpool had overlooked. My argument that I was to meet Dr Peter Heuith, one of France's most eminent dentists, who would vouch for me, cut no ice, nor did the fact that I was just passing through for one night. It was not until a businessman quietly suggested that I ask for a 24-hour shoppers' visa that the difficulty was resolved.

It was not the first nor the last time I had trouble at Charles de Gaulle. My Rhodesian/Zimbabwe passport often caused problems and kept the Liverpool team waiting while I stood in a separate queue. It even happened on the way out to Rome for the European Cup Final, when I had to transfer at the major Paris airport. No doubt it won't be the last time, and hopefully I won't be replaced with a keeper before I have a chance to catch up with the team!